Monologue
Mastery

Monologue Mastery

How to Find and Perform the Perfect Monologue

Prudence Wright Holmes

An Imprint of Hal Leonard Corporation
New York

Published in 2010 by Limelight Editions
An Imprint of Hal Leonard Corporation
7777 West Bluemound Road
Milwaukee, WI 53213

Trade Book Division Editorial Offices
19 West 21st Street, New York, NY 10010

Printed in the United States of America

Book design by Publishers' Design and Production Services, Inc.

Library of Congress Cataloging-in-Publication Data

Holmes, Prudence.
  Monologue mastery : how to find and perform the perfect monologue / Prudence Wright Holmes.
     p. cm.
  Includes bibliographical references.
  ISBN 978-0-87910-370-5
  1. Acting--Auditions. 2. Monologues. I. Title.
  PN2071.A92H585 2010
  792.02'8--dc22
                              2010000312

www.limelighteditions.com

Contents

Preface

They call me "The Monologue Detective." I've been helping actors find monologues and coaching them for auditions for over twenty-five years.

In this book, I'm going to share with you the secrets of doing a successful monologue audition. You will learn how and where to find little-known monologues that fit you like a glove. You will also learn how to get them ready for auditions.

I'm an actor myself. I've been in the business for over thirty years. I know what it's like to be out there auditioning and struggling with monologues. I used to be very frightened of doing monologues. Now I enjoy them. You can, too. If you have a monologue that fits you perfectly and you act it well, you will start to get good feedback at auditions. Then you will want to go to them more often, just to have a chance to work out.

I created this book to give you a step-by-step process to help you to get positive results at auditions when you are asked to do monologues.

Several years ago, there was a place in New York City (where I live) called The Actor's Information Project. They taught actors the business of show business. Casting directors and agents came in and gave seminars in which everyone had to do a monologue. I went to these seminars, and I got to see other actors' monologues. I was really shocked when I saw what some of them had picked as their choice of material.

It seemed like they had no sense of who they were and what kind of material was appropriate for them. For example, a beautiful, statuesque model chose a monologue from *The Woolgatherer*. Her character was a shy wallflower who had never had a date. An elderly man of seventy chose to play Benedick, the romantic lead from *Much Ado About Nothing*. When I saw these poor choices of material, I thought to myself, "These people need more appropriate monologues if they want to get the job."

I had always liked to read, so I knew many plays. Also, I had good intuition regarding what monologues would be appropriate for the actors in the seminars. So one day, I suggested to the model that she do a monologue from *American Dreams*, a book by Studs Terkel. The character was a former Miss USA. A few weeks later, I saw her do this piece. I was amazed that simply by changing her material a real miracle had happened. Suddenly, she looked as if she was much more talented. Then I approached the older man who had done *Much Ado About Nothing*. I suggested he do a monologue from *Scenes from American Life* by A. R. Gurney. He did, and he also seemed transformed into a much better actor.

I realized I was on to something. So I began doing this professionally. I have helped thousands of actors get agents, jobs, and to have more successful auditions. My clients have appeared in feature films, prime-time television, on and off Broadway, regional theatres, soap operas, and commercials.

I have also maintained a successful acting career. I have appeared on Broadway four times, have had featured roles in seven films, and a recurring role on a soap opera. I've performed at many regional and off-Broadway theatres and written and performed my solo show, *Bexley, Oh!* at the New York Theatre Workshop. I have also done hundreds of television commercials. I performed monologues in order to get many of these jobs.

I get phone calls every day from people who want private coaching. They tell me horror stories about how they've been to the bookstore, and they've spent hundreds of dollars on plays and monologue books. But they still can't find a monologue they like.

For me, it's easier, because I'm just looking for good monologues and waiting for the right person to come along. For you, the search is a little narrower, because you're dealing with only one person with very specific needs.

In order to have a successful audition experience, three things have to happen:

First: Your monologue should be little known.

Second: It should fit you perfectly and show the auditors how you can be cast.

Third: You should act the monologue really well.

In the following chapters, I am going to discuss each of these three areas in detail.

CHAPTER ONE

Finding Little-Known Monologues

I FIRMLY BELIEVE THAT IT IS IMPORTANT to have a monologue that the auditors haven't heard ten other people perform. If you're doing the tenth version of *A Boy's Life* or *A . . . My Name is Alice* that the auditors have heard that day, they're not going to be too excited about the prospect of hearing that piece yet again. In fact, one student of mine told me that she did a monologue from *A . . . My Name is Alice* at an audition and she forgot the words. However, the auditor knew it by heart since he had heard it so often. So he gave her the next line.

Many agents and casting directors have told me that they make their decision about an actor within the first ten seconds of meeting them. If you come in and tell them, "My monologue is from *Crimes of the Heart* [or *Nuts*, or some other overdone monologue]," many auditors will turn off to you immediately. It's unfortunate, because you might have a brilliant rendition of one of those pieces, but some auditors often have very closed minds. They just don't want to hear that same monologue again.

I can sympathize with them. They're sitting there eight hours a day; every five minutes a new person comes in and often does a monologue that they have heard many times before. It's hard for them to be interested after a while unless you do something to capture their attention.

It can be very boring because many actors are not that compelling to watch. Part of your job at the audition is to wake them up. You have to try to get their attention immediately. If your big moment comes halfway through your piece, they probably won't even be listening to you by that time.

In the back of this book is a list of monologues that are done frequently and should be avoided.

In searching for little-known monologues, there are many places that you can look.

Plays and Films

As you begin your monologue search, first read and attend plays and films. That's pretty obvious. I hope most of you do that whenever you can. You should become familiar with the works of all the great playwrights such as Shakespeare, Molière, Arthur Miller, Tennessee Williams, and Eugene O'Neill. Start by reading their major works and then read their lesser-known plays. These can often be excellent sources of material because they are rarely performed. And yet the writing is still very good.

Immerse yourself in the world of the performing arts. Check out DVDs from the library. Begin with some of the great classic films by brilliant directors such as Orson Welles or Francis Ford Coppola. As you did with the plays, see these directors' big hits first, then check out their flops for monologue material.

Workshops and Readings

Going to workshops and readings is an especially good idea because the playwright usually attends these performances. Ask the theatre staff if the playwright is there. If so, have them point the playwright out to you. When you meet him or her, say you liked the play and ask for a copy. Many playwrights are very flattered if you want to do a monologue from their play, especially if they are not that well known. It's a chance for them to have people in the business see their material performed, even if it's only a three-minute monologue.

If the playwright isn't there, you can find out the name of the playwright's agent and contact that person. Many times, they'll even give you a copy of the play for free. If you hear something you think would be appropriate for you in a reading, track it down. Probably nobody else is doing it.

A student of mine ran into the playwright John Guare on the street. She went up to him and said, "Oh, Mr. Guare, I love your work. I'm doing one of your monologues. And it is so wonderful."

He invited her for tea.

Then she said, "Do have any other plays or monologues that are not published?"

So he let her look at some of his unpublished and out-of-print scripts. She got some really good material.

Plays of Other Eras

Plays of other eras are also good sources of monologues because many of them are rarely done; however, they can be somewhat dated. You have to examine them closely to make sure that they work in this day and age. Sometimes they have references to people and things that we don't understand today.

A student of mine did a monologue from *The Man Who Came to Dinner*. There was a character named Lorraine who was always name-dropping. The people she referred to were very famous in the nineteen thirties. But people today wouldn't know who they were. So I helped her to update the monologue and substitute people who were the modern-day equivalent of those people from the thirties.

Other Literary Sources

Other good places to find little-known monologues are autobiographies, novels, short stories, and magazine articles written in the first person.

I subscribe to certain magazines because they have excerpts from books. Often, these publications have edited versions of many famous peoples' autobiographies. One of my favorite magazines is *People*. They tend to excerpt the most dramatic parts of books.

I made a monologue from an excerpt from a book in *People* by Benazir Bhutto, the former Prime Minister of Pakistan. Her father was also the Prime Minister, Ali Bhutto. He was thrown in jail by his enemies and executed. She and her whole family were also thrown in jail. Next, her brother was poisoned. Another brother was shot to death. Benazir was accused of orchestrating it. Her husband was put in jail. Benazir Bhutto's life was just one drama after another right up to her unfortunate assassination.

The monologue I found was about her saying good-by to her father just before he's executed. It's incredibly powerful. Another monologue from *People* was the true story of an actor on *One Life to Live* who was being stalked by a crazy man. She finally had to leave the soap opera and go into hiding because she was afraid for her life.

Reader's Digest can be a good source of material. They have this feature every month called "Drama in Real Life." There was one story about a man who is on a camping trip. A bear attacks him and snatches off his scalp. He walks ten miles with his scalp in his hands to the hospital. It's very dramatic.

Reader's Digest also publishes excerpts from books, and these can be good sources of monologue material. It also saves time to go to sources like these, because then you don't have to read the whole book.

There are so many books, novels and autobiographies where you can find material. I've taken material from books by Studs Terkel, Garrison Keillor, Jay McInerney, Carrie Fisher, and others.

Start reading the book review sections of *The New York Times* and other papers, and see what's out there. If a book has a character that you think you might be able to play, read that book. You may discover a book by a writer who really speaks to you or mirrors your life experiences in some way. In that case, read everything that writer has ever written. It could be a great source for you. Some of my students have even created one-person shows this way. Check out the letters to the editor, "Dear Abby," and the editorial pages of newspapers, too.

There was once a great editorial in *The New York Times* written by Maureen Dowd. She wrote in the first person as if she were Monica Lewinsky. In this piece, she was trying to pitch a book about her affair with President Clinton. Maureen Dowd happens to be one of my favorite columnists. She has written other columns in the first person, too. There was one in which she pretended to be Clinton, telling his side of the Lewinsky affair, and another one in which she pretended to be Al Gore complaining that he was really a fun guy and nobody realized it. It was very funny. Since Maureen Dowd won a Pulitzer Prize, you can be assured that her writing is very good.

I have also looked in other places in *The New York Times* such as "Modern Love" in the Styles section and the last page of the Magazine section of the Sunday *Times*. Sometimes you can find good monologue material there as well.

Audio Books

Another favorite monologue source that I often use is audio books. I'm always listening to audio books on my iPod at the gym when I'm working out, on car trips, and when I'm doing my taxes. You can get them from the library. Audio books are usually abridged. The editors tend to pick the high points. I like the high points, because those are the most dramatic parts of the story and tend to make the most interesting monologues.

I just listened to Christopher Reeve's audio book. He talked about his riding accident, his life-and-death struggle after it occurred. It was really very touching and would make an excellent monologue. Roseanne Barr has an audio book that is also very entertaining.

Film and TV Scripts

There's a company in LA called Script City, which has scripts of many TV shows, movies of the week, and just about everything that's on television except news and documentaries. You can order scripts from them if you are unable to get a recording of the show. It can be a bit more costly, but it may be worth it if you can't find the material any other way. Check them out at www.scriptcity.com, 800-676-2522.

Become a Reader

Another good idea for finding monologue material is to be a reader. By doing this, you get in on all the first rounds of auditions, before the play has been done if it's a new play. Frequently, you can get material from the auditors if you see something that you like.

Being a reader is a great thing anyway because it puts you on the same level as the casting directors. You become one of them. You can also learn a lot. Ted Danson was a reader when he first went to Hollywood, and that's how he got to know a lot of producers and writers. They liked him so much that they ended up writing *Cheers* with him in mind. It's really good to just get out there and get to know people. Call casting directors and ask to be put on their reader's list. Not only is it a great learning experience, but also you get paid for it.

The Internet

There are many monologue Web sites on the Worldwide Web. Although there are too many to list here, the general rule when searching the Web for monologues is to focus on writers who have been paid for their work or who have received some kind of award or have had a production of their play. Then you increase your chances that the writing will be high quality and show you off well. You can also find movie scripts at Drew's Script-o-Rama—www.script-o-rama.com. Here you have access to thousands of screenplays. Check out these kinds of sources instead of a Website created by someone with no track record. If you go to a search engine, such as Google, and type in "monologues," you will get thousands of matches.

Many of these will be companies selling books or some people who think they can write. In this case, proceed with caution. Remember that bad writing makes you look bad.

Monologue Books

Some of the same principles used in searching the Web also apply to monologue books. I generally advise students to go to other sources because monologue books are the first places most actors look. So the material in them tends to get overdone. However, if you do use a monologue book, make sure it has excerpts from plays that have been performed or published. In general, monologue books in which one person writes all the selections are not good sources of material. There is no play for you to refer to in order to get information about your character.

Remember, a good writer will make your job easier. The lines will make sense and feel natural. You will be able to figure out the character's motivation quickly. You will want to go to auditions and speak those lines. You will not often feel that way about a monologue written by someone who is not a professional.

Auditions

Always be on the lookout for good monologues. Often, when you're at auditions, you see a table with scenes or monologues for the actors who are auditioning. Look at all of them. If you see a good monologue, ask if you can take a copy for your files. Many times, you can find some very interesting material this way.

Writing Your Own Monologues

Many actors ask me if it's okay to write their own monologues. I think you have to take a long, hard look at your talent before you decide that you're going to write a monologue for yourself.

An agent at a well-known agency here in New York has audition nights where people come in and do monologues. She said they can usually tell when people have written their own monologue because the writing is not very good. The auditors even have a code that they write on actors' cards when they do monologues that they have written themselves. Most of the time, in her opinion, this is not a good thing. She feels the material is usually not professional.

Most people can't write as well as John Guare, John Patrick Shanley, or Tina Howe. This is what these people do for a living. They've been paid for their services, so they have more credibility, more skill.

I've had some people come and work with me who've written their own material. I've had to let them down gently. I tell them that it's just not showing them off well. Often, it sounds too "written." It's not the way people talk. It's too descriptive. Or it's not that dramatic. Or the truth is the writing is not very good. You walk a slippery slope when you write your own monologue. If you tell an agent you wrote it, he may think you're not really acting; it's just you playing yourself. If you decide to do something you wrote yourself, give yourself a pen name.

I've even talked to actors who say, "I'll just go in there and make something up on the spur of the moment."

They actually think they're going to come across looking like a professional. The chances are a million to one that that will happen.

But I don't want to discourage any would-be writers. If you really feel that you're a great writer and you can show yourself off well with your writing, I think you should give it a try and see what kind of feedback you get. Here are some exercises that will help you create your own monologue.

EXERCISE

Use a voice recorder to record the following exercises:

1. Talk to a friend about a subject you feel passionate about.
2. Tell your friend a story of an event you feel strongly about.
3. Imitate a person you know who you think is an interesting character.
4. Create a situation, either from your life or from your imagination, in which you are fighting hard to get what you want.

When you have finished these exercises, type up what's on your recording device. Then edit it down and shape it into a monologue. Make sure it's dramatic and not too narrative or descriptive. Also, structure it so that it tells a coherent story and has a beginning, a middle, and an end.

Exceptions to the Rules

When it comes to little-known monologues, I always like to mention the exceptions to the rules. Acting isn't like computer programming where, if you push F7, the same thing will always happen. This is a business where creativity counts. Sometimes breaking the rules will work. Then again, sometimes it won't.

When I was going to casting workshops at The Actor's Information Project, there was a woman who came in one night and did a monologue from a Tough Love meeting. She had gone to a meeting with a tape recorder, unbeknownst to the other participants who thought they were speaking confidentially, and taped their comments. So this woman did a monologue of a person who had a troubled teenage daughter who was on drugs. It was really boring. It just wasn't dramatic. The writing was rambling and very self-indulgent.

That same night, another person got up and did a monologue that I personally had heard at least three or four times. The auditor had also heard it before. But that actor made us forget this because her take on it was so different and so interesting.

So that's something to consider. If you really feel you're the perfect Hamlet or the perfect Tom in *The Glass Menagerie*, and you can make the auditors forget all those other people they've seen do those pieces, then you should have it in your repertoire. But you should have other monologues as well.

If you go to these little-known sources, you will be more likely to find material that will make the auditors sit up and take notice of you.

Summary

Sources of good, little-known monologues include:

1. Lesser-known works of well-known playwrights
2. Plays of other eras
3. Workshops and readings

4. Other literary sources such as books, magazines, and newspaper articles
5. Audio books
6. Being a reader
7. TV and film scripts
8. Book clubs
9. The Internet
10. Monologue books
11. Auditions
12. Your own written material

CHAPTER TWO

Discovering Your Unique Qualities

Now we're going to talk about how to discover what's special about you. I have given you suggestions about how and where to find little-known monologues. Let's figure out how to tell what roles are right for you.

Who Are You?

It is often hard to be objective about yourself. When I work with people individually, I send them a questionnaire in advance. See this questionnaire below and fill it out.

Questionnaire

1. Where are you from?

2. How do people describe your personality? (include positive and negative qualities)

3. Typecast yourself (for example, the best friend, the villain).

4. Is there are role you have always wanted to play or people have said you should play?

5. What is your favorite role you have played and why?

6. Who are your favorite playwrights?

7. Describe your ideal monologue.

8. Do you have any issues, problems, or conflicts in your life that you would relate to in a monologue?

9. What is your age and age range?

10. Describe your family background. What were your parents like? What were their professions?

11. Have you ever been compared to anyone famous? Who?

12. How are you cast most often?

13. What monologues are you doing now? Why did you choose them?

14. Is there any subject or type of monologue that you want to avoid?

Take a Survey

If you had trouble filling out the questionnaire, ask your friends, families, teachers, and directors to give you their opinions of you. You have to think of yourself as a product. Any time a company is bringing out a new product, they do market research. They have focus groups. They ask people to describe their product and tell them what they like or don't like about it. You have to conduct your own focus group on your product, which is yourself, and get a variety of opinions from people as to how they see you. After a while, you will come up with a consensus. Maybe people tell you that you seem like the girl next door type. Maybe they say you have an edge that would make you believable as a villain. This is all useful information that will guide you in your search for monologues.

Problems and Conflicts

On the questionnaire, I ask, "Do you have any issues, problems, or conflicts in your life that you would relate to in a monologue?"

I ask about problems and conflicts because that's what they write plays about. They don't write them about your trip to the grocery store, unless something dramatic happens on that trip.

Often, students answer my question about problems in this way: "I didn't get along with my father, so I could relate to a monologue about someone confronting his father."

Or a student might tell me," I have an alcoholic mother."

Another person may say," I'm really into social issues. I relate to monologues about the rights of downtrodden people."

If you have had a life with many traumas, maybe you're lucky. Pat Conroy, who wrote *Prince of Tides*, once said that having an unhappy childhood is the greatest gift a writer can receive. The same thing is true for actors. If you've been through hell, count your blessings because now you can relate to characters in plays with similar experiences, like Blanche DuBois in *A Streetcar Named Desire*. If your life has been a bed of roses, it's harder to identify with those great dramatic roles. I'm not encouraging you to create problems in your life just so you can portray them on stage. Don't be like Vivien Leigh, who played a character with tuberculosis and then contracted the disease. But if you have had a rough time in life, at least put your experiences to good use on stage. Acting can be very therapeutic and even healing.

Age

Many actors are understandably sensitive about the question of age. At an audition, you should never tell them how old you are. You should not put that information on your resume either. In fact, it's against the law for employers to ask your age. If you are asked, make light of it and reply, "What age are you looking for?" Or you might say, "My age range is twenty-eight to thirty-two." If you do give an age range, limit it to a few years. Saying that you can play any age between twenty and forty is not realistic.

Remember, if you're thirty-five and do a monologue written for someone who's a teenager, you will be competing against real teenagers. And they will be more believable as that age than you will be.

The reason you should not answer the age question is not out of vanity. It's because you don't want to give them any reason to turn you down for the job. If they're looking for someone who is twenty-five and you tell them you are thirty, they may say you are too old without even giving you a chance. Many times casting people are entirely too literal when it comes to age.

On my questionnaire, I want you to tell the truth about your age. It will help you to figure out what types of monologues are right for you. Without fail, everyone gives me the same answer to this question: "I am __ years old, but everybody says I look much younger." We all want to look younger. But let's be honest. Most people look their age, give or take a few years. You are doing yourself a disservice by doing monologues that are too young for you.

Conversely, many young actors want to tackle roles that are too old for them because they are juicy parts. I know that Blanche DuBois is one of the great acting roles of all time, but most women in their twenties can't pull it off. That doesn't stop many of them from trying. If you want to work on it in your acting class, fine. Just don't do it at an audition.

Occasionally, I will work with an actor who is young but has had such a troubled life that she can relate to a complex, older character like Martha in *Who's Afraid of Virginia Woolf?* That kind of person may be able to get away with doing this role, but I would still encourage her to look for similar roles in her own age category.

Also, there are some roles written for very young characters that are so difficult that only an older actor could pull them off— for example, the role of Frankie in Carson McCullers' play *The Member of the Wedding*. Although she is only twelve, Frankie must have an incredible emotional depth and range. For this reason, the role is often cast with an older actor.

George Bernard Shaw once said, "There are no great Juliets under forty." We have seen some younger actors succeed with this role in recent years, but the point is, often, younger people have not had the life experiences to do justice to this role.

Act What You Know

Writers also often follow the rule "Write what you know" with great success. I would suggest that you act what you know. It will make it much easier for you to relate to a character if you have had a similar experience. But don't get carried away. I once gave a monologue to one of my students in which the character talks about once going on a picnic with his father when he was a child.

My student said, "I can't do this monologue. I never went on a picnic with my father."

Don't be so literal in your choice of material. You'll never find a monologue which is exactly like your life story, but you can find monologues that embody your emotional experiences. Some actors get so picky about finding a monologue that is totally perfect for them that they never do anything. I have had actors say to me, "I want a monologue that's really funny but at the same time incredibly tragic. I want to be very strong yet weak. I would also be good if I could be suffering from a fatal disease and have an incestuous relationship with my father and be from Texas because that's where I'm from." Your goal is to get in the right ballpark, but you don't have to find a piece that completely mirrors your life. That is nearly impossible.

There also seems to be a trend among young women right now: they want to play strong women. They often tell me they don't want to play victims or anyone vulnerable. They don't realize that these kinds of parts often show their emotional abilities better than a monologue of some alpha woman.

Sometimes, you may not be that drawn to your monologue when you read it to yourself. Try reading it out loud or to a friend. Some monologues may not seem that exciting on the printed page, but they really come to life when you get on your feet and act them. Keep an open mind.

Typecasting Yourself

Many well-known actors have focused on what they do best. And they've taken it all the way to the bank. Al Pacino is always the intense, ethnic guy. Goldie Hawn is always the silly one. They've tried to go outside of those kinds of roles occasionally, and they haven't succeeded. Al Pacino tried to be a soldier in the Revolutionary War. It just didn't work. Goldie Hawn did a drama, but her fans didn't go to see it.

In Julia Cameron's book *The Vein of Gold*, which is the sequel to *The Artist's Way*, Martin Scorsese said, "Every actor needs to find his vein of gold." He used Robert De Niro as an example. He said, "Romantic love is not De Niro's vein of gold—but male bonding is." He felt De Niro had found his vein of gold in those tough characters.

So I encourage you all to try to find your vein of gold and really make it work for you.

Many actors say to me, "But I'm versatile. I can play a bag woman. I can be eighty years old. I can be a debutante. I can be everything."

Well, maybe you can, but not at your first audition. To get your foot in the door, do what you do best.

If you try to be all things to all people, I think you'll end up confusing the agent or casting person, especially initially. Whether you like it or not, there's something called typecasting. The minute you walk in the door, they make decisions about you. Sometimes they decide that they don't want you before you even speak. They want someone taller, or they want someone with blonde hair.

You can't control some of the reasons why they don't choose you for the part. That's why you should focus on perfecting those things that are under your control.

Influences That Shaped You

In trying to figure out what monologues are right for you, it's often helpful to put yourself under a microscope and study who you are. One good way to do that is to write your autobiography. It doesn't have to be long. You will get an idea of what kind of subjects you have special knowledge of. Are you from the South? If so, you might want to have a Southern monologue in your repertoire. Although I don't think that's the only type of monologue you should do. But if you're from the South or New England or New York, you should have one of those monologues in your back pocket.

Notice, as you write your autobiography, what kind of influences shaped you. That will give you a clue as to where to look for material. Here are some exercises that will help you.

EXERCISE

Write your autobiography.

1. Where are you from?
2. Describe your childhood.
3. What were your parents like?
4. Describe a time when you felt very sad.
5. Describe the happiest time of your childhood.
6. Remember a fight you had.
7. Remember your first romantic relationship.

Researching Actors Like You

Research actors you've been compared to. If you are told you look like a well-known actor, look that person up on the International Movie Data Base (www.imdb.com) or the International Broadway Data Base (www.ibdb.com) on the internet. Study his or her credits. Also, many video guides list thousands of actors and their credits in the appendix. See what roles he or she has done. Then you can either rent that movie or read that play and see if there are any monologues or speeches that you can piece together to make a monologue.

Another good idea when researching actors you've been compared to is to find out what actors *they* have been compared to and research those actors as well.

Feedback from Strangers

EXERCISE

Go with a partner to the airport or the bus terminal. Have your partner stand by a post or sit in a chair. Go up to a stranger and say, "You see that person over there by the post? How would you describe him or her?"

To help you with this exercise, here's a list of descriptive words that might be useful. If the person has trouble, just ask him or her to check off which words apply. If you don't want to go to a public place, you can also do this with someone you meet for the first time.

DESCRIPTIVE WORDS

Aggressive	From the country	Scandinavian
Airhead	Funny	Scary
Anal	Happy	Sexy
Asian	Haughty	Slick
British	Hick	Sloppy
Calm	Hip	Smart
Charming	Innocent	Sophisticated
Childlike	Intense	Spanish
Clever	Italian	Spoiled brat
Cold	Jewish	Suburban
Con artist	Laid back	Timid
Crazy	Mean	Tough
Dangerous	Middle Eastern	Urban
Earthy	Middle European	Vulnerable
Elegant	Nerd	Warm
Ethereal	Neurotic	Waspy
Exotic	Professional	Wealthy
Fragile	Quirky	
From another era	Sarcastic	

It's amazing how many times a complete stranger, without even hearing a person speak, will be quite accurate in his description of them. We are all giving off signals about ourselves all the time. You've got to make it your mission to find out who you are and what you do best.

Updating Your Product

Of course, as we get older, we all change. So, you have to update your monologues just as you update your picture and resume. You've got to keep getting feedback, keep getting new monologues that are more appropriate to you as you move into different age categories. Or you may simply get tired of a piece after a few months. If you feel it's losing its immediacy, retire it for a while and learn a new one. You must constantly be on top of things.

Remember that show business is a *business*. Just as the auto industry comes out with new models every year, you should also update your product every year or so. Get a new hairstyle, new clothes, new pictures, and new monologues.

Fantasizing About Your Ideal Role

EXERCISE

Daydream about what kind of role you'd be really great at. Picture what your character looks like. How does he/she speak? What place do you picture your character in? How does he or she dress? What subject would your character talk about? Write it down in your journal, and keep a record of that. It will give you information from your subconscious about what kind of characters you feel drawn to.

Review Your Resume

After doing all these exercises, review your resume. See how you have been cast. Are there any trends? Do you always play the leading man or are you a character actor? If you've gotten work consistently doing a certain kind of part, then look for that kind of monologue.

Breaking the Rules

Now I would like to talk about the exceptions to the rule. There are people, few and far between, who do monologues that are really not right for them, and yet it works for them.

I remember this Asian actor I knew who had an audition for a Broadway show. He was asked to do a monologue. This was right at the height of the *Miss Saigon* controversy. Asian actors were picketing because a non-Asian actor was cast as an Asian in a leading role. Everyone was being very politically correct. In spite of this, the Asian actor chose as his monologue a highly dramatic speech from *Othello*. He was completely wrong for the part, as Othello is supposed to be a large black man. But he really wanted to play Othello, even though he was 5'2" and Asian. He went to the audition, which was on the stage at a Broadway theater. He did this very dramatic monologue of Othello killing Desdemona.

When it was over, there was complete silence. Then the director's voice came from the back of the theater, "Oh, that was very bold of you." And he got the job.

Race

The issue of race is a very sensitive one. If you are an ethnic minority, do all you can to open the auditors' minds to nontraditional casting. Audition for every role you think you are right for, regardless of the character's race. Unfortunately, some auditors will resist this. Most of the time, nontraditional casting can bring a fresh interpretation to a role; however, it won't always work. For example, if you're a black female, I wouldn't suggest doing the role of Miss Daisy in *Driving Miss Daisy*. This play concerns the relationship of a white Southern woman with her black chauffeur. It wouldn't make sense if Miss Daisy were a black woman.

If you are a Caucasian actor, I would advise you not to do a role specifically written for an Asian, African American, or other ethnic minority. A white female student of mine once did Rose's monologue from *Fences* at an audition. There were some African American auditors in the room. The response was chilly.

They said, "Why did you choose that monologue?" The implication was that since there are so many monologues written for white actors, why did this actor have to do one specifically written for a black character?

In Conclusion

I strongly recommend trying to gather as many opinions about yourself and roles that you are right for as you possibly can. Put yourself under a microscope. Making a study of what it is that you do best will help you to make more informed choices of monologue material.

If all else fails, take a look at yourself in the mirror. Honestly assess what you look like. It's a good place to start. I know everyone wants to think of himself or herself as young and beautiful, but only a small minority of actors actually are. If you are forty pounds overweight, don't do a monologue that would be right for Angelina Jolie. Whoever you are, celebrate it. Actors like Kathy Bates and Philip Seymour Hoffman have had very successful careers even though they are not glamorous.

This same principle goes for your pictures as well. Many photographers will want to put too much makeup on their female clients and have them wear sexy clothes. Don't let them do this to you if this is not how you are usually cast. In fact, if you play blue-collar types, have some pictures taken without any makeup at all.

When you have a clear idea of who you are and what you're selling, you will be more likely to choose monologues that really work for you.

Summary

Figure out which monologues are right for you by taking the following steps:

1. Fill out and study the questionnaire on pages 11–13.
2. Act what you know.
3. Typecast yourself.
4. Write your autobiography.
5. Research actors you've been compared to.
6. Get feedback from strangers.
7. Update your monologues frequently.
8. Fantasize about your ideal role.
9. Review your resume.
10. Consider your age, race, and physical appearance.
11. Dare to break the rules occasionally.

CHAPTER THREE

Shaping Your Monologue

As I have said, I often take monologues from books and magazine articles. But I also piece them together from scenes in plays or films. I simply eliminate the other character. After I've done this, if there are any lines that don't make sense, I cut them. However, in piecing together monologues from scenes or other sources, there are a number of things to keep in mind.

Hit the High Points

You have to look at your piece and try to determine what are the funniest or the most dramatic parts. Then you should shape it so that it has a beginning, a middle, and an end. Sometimes, you may have to do a little rewriting to make the piece flow better. Don't be afraid to take lines from different scenes and combine them to make a monologue. Just be sure it makes sense.

Let's look at how to create a monologue from a literary source.

We will use a portion of the text from *Jane Eyre* by Charlotte Brontë. The lines to use in the monologue are in bold. In this speech, Rochester confesses the truth to Jane about his secret wife and the hell he has been going through ever since her madness began.

"**Jane,** I will not trouble you with abominable details: some strong words shall express what I have to say. **I lived with that woman upstairs four years, and before that time she had tried me indeed: her character ripened and developed with frightful rapidity; her vices sprang up fast and rank: they were so strong, only cruelty could check them, and I would not use cruelty. What a pigmy intellect she had— and what giant propensities! How fearful were the curses those propensities entailed on me! Bertha Mason, the true daughter of an infamous mother, dragged me through all the hideous and degrading agonies which must attend a man bound to a wife at once intemperate and unchaste.**

"My brother in the interval was dead, and at the end of the four years my father died too. I was rich enough now—yet poor to hideous indigence: a nature the most gross, impure, depraved I ever saw, was associated with mine, and called by the law and by society a part of me. And I could not rid myself of it by any legal proceedings: for the doctors now discovered that *my wife* was mad—her excesses had prematurely developed the germs of insanity. Jane, you don't like my narrative; you look almost sick—shall I defer the rest to another day?"

"No, sir, finish it now; I pity you—I do earnestly pity you."

"Pity, Jane, from some people is a noxious and insulting sort of tribute, which one is justified in hurling back in the teeth of those who offer it; but that is the sort of pity native to callous, selfish hearts; it is a hybrid, egotistical pain at hearing of woes, crossed with ignorant contempt for those who have endured them. But that is not your pity, Jane; it is not the feeling of which your whole face is full at this moment—with which your eyes are now almost overflowing—with which your heart is heaving—with which your hand is trembling in mine. Your pity, my darling, is the suffering mother of love: its anguish is the very natal pang of the divine passion. I accept it, Jane; let the daughter have free advent—my arms wait to receive her."

"Now, sir, proceed; what did you do when you found she was mad?"

"**Jane, I approached the verge of despair; a remnant of self-respect was all that intervened between me and the** gulf. In the eyes of the world, I was doubtless covered with grimy dishonour; but I resolved to be clean in my own sight—and to the last I repudiated the contamination of her crimes, and wrenched myself from connection with her mental defects. Still, society associated my name and person with hers; I yet saw her and heard her daily: something of her breath (faugh!) mixed with the air I breathed; and besides, I remembered I had once been her husband—that recollection was then, and is now, inexpressibly odious to me; moreover, I knew that while she lived I could never be the husband of another and better wife; and, though five years my senior (her family and her father had lied to me even in the particular of her age), she was likely to live as long as I, being as robust in frame as she was infirm in mind. Thus, at the age of twenty-six, I was hopeless.

"One night I had been awakened by her yells—(since the medical men had pronounced her mad, she had, of course, been shut up)—it was a fiery West Indian night; one of the description that frequently precedes the hurricanes of those climates. Being unable to sleep in bed, I got up and opened the window. The air was like sulphur-steams—I could find no refreshment anywhere. Mosquitoes came buzzing in and hummed sullenly round the room; the sea, which I could hear from thence, rumbled dull like an earthquake—black clouds were casting up over it; the moon was setting in the waves, broad and red, like a hot cannon-ball—she threw her last bloody glance over a world quivering with the ferment of tempest. I was physically influenced by the atmosphere and scene, and my ears were filled with the curses the maniac still shrieked out; wherein she momentarily mingled my name with such a tone of demon-hate, with such language!—no professed harlot ever had a fouler vocabulary than she: though two rooms off, I heard every word—the thin partitions of the West India house opposing but slight obstruction to her wolfish cries.

"'This life,' said I at last, 'is hell! this is the air—those are the sounds of the bottomless pit! I have a right to deliver myself from it if I can. The sufferings of this mortal state will leave me with the heavy flesh that now cumbers my soul. Of the fanatic's burning eternity I have no fear:

there is not a future state worse than this present one—let
me break away and go home to God!'

Now let's make the speech into a shorter monologue, using
the sections in bold.

"Jane, I lived with that woman upstairs four years, and before that time she had tried me indeed: her character ripened and developed with frightful rapidity; her vices sprang
up fast and rank: they were so strong, only cruelty could
check them, and I would not use cruelty. What a pigmy intellect she had—and what giant propensities! How fearful
were the curses those propensities entailed on me! Bertha
Mason, the true daughter of an infamous mother, dragged
me through all the hideous and degrading agonies which
must attend a man bound to a wife at once intemperate and
unchaste.
      "Jane, I approached the verge of despair; a remnant of
self-respect was all that intervened between me and the gulf.
In the eyes of the world, I was doubtless covered with grimy
dishonour; but I resolved to be clean in my own sight--and
to the last I repudiated the contamination of her crimes,
and wrenched myself from connection with her mental defects. One night I had been awakened by her yells—it was
a fiery West Indian night; one of the description that frequently precedes the hurricanes of those climates. Being
unable to sleep in bed, I got up and opened the window.
The air was like sulphur-steams—I could find no refreshment anywhere. Mosquitoes came buzzing in and hummed
sullenly round the room; the sea, which I could hear from
thence, rumbled dull like an earthquake--black clouds were
casting up over it; the moon was setting in the waves, broad
and red, like a hot cannon-ball—she threw her last bloody
glance over a world quivering with the ferment of tempest. I
was physically influenced by the atmosphere and scene, and
my ears were filled with the curses the maniac still shrieked
out; wherein she momentarily mingled my name with such
a tone of demon-hate, with such language!—no professed
harlot ever had a fouler vocabulary than she: though two

rooms off, I heard every word—the thin partitions of the West India house opposing but slight obstruction to her wolfish cries.

"'This life,' said I at last, 'is hell! this is the air—those are the sounds of the bottomless pit! I have a right to deliver myself from it if I can. The sufferings of this mortal state will leave me with the heavy flesh that now cumbers my soul. Of the fanatic's burning eternity I have no fear: there is not a future state worse than this present one—let me break away and go home to God!'"

I have deleted references to people and events that the auditors might not understand. I have also removed all extraneous dialogue that does not move the monologue forward. Now we can focus on Rochester's anguished confession to Jane more easily.

Here is a section of *Wuthering Heights* by Emily Brontë that can easily be made into a monologue. As Catherine is dying from complications with her pregnancy, she pours her heart out to Heathcliff, forgiving and condemning him for all that has gone on between them.

"Oh, Cathy! Oh, my life! how can I bear it?" was the first sentence he uttered, in a tone that did not seek to disguise his despair. And now he stared at her so earnestly that I thought the very intensity of his gaze would bring tears into his eyes; but they burned with anguish: they did not melt.

"What now?" said Catherine, leaning back, and returning his look with a suddenly clouded brow: her humour was a mere vane for constantly varying caprices. **You and Edgar have broken my heart, Heathcliff! And you both come to bewail the deed to me, as if *you* were the people to be pitied! I shall not pity you, not I. You have killed me—and thriven on it, I think. How strong you are! How many years do you mean to live after I am gone?"**

Heathcliff had knelt on one knee to embrace her; he attempted to rise, but she seized his hair, and kept him down.

"**I wish I could hold you,**" she continued, bitterly, "**till we were both dead! I shouldn't care what you suffered. I** care nothing for your sufferings. Why shouldn't you suffer? I do! Will you forget me? Will you be happy when I am in the earth? Will you say twenty years hence, 'That's the grave of Catherine Earnshaw? I loved her long ago, and was wretched to lose her; but it is past. I've loved many others since: my children are dearer to me than she was; and, at death, I shall not rejoice that I am going to her: I shall be sorry that I must leave them!' Will you say so, Heathcliff?"

"Don't torture me till I'm as mad as yourself," cried he, wrenching his head free, and grinding his teeth.

The two, to a cool spectator, made a strange and fearful picture. Well might Catherine deem that heaven would be a land of exile to her, unless with her mortal body she cast away her moral character also. Her present countenance had a wild vindictiveness in its white cheek, and a bloodless lip and scintillating eye; and she retained in her closed fingers a portion of the locks she had been grasping. As to her companion, while raising himself with one hand, he had taken her arm with the other; and so inadequate was his stock of gentleness to the requirements of her condition, that on his letting go I saw four distinct impressions left blue in the colourless skin.

"Are you possessed with a devil," he pursued, savagely, "to talk in that manner to me when you are dying? Do you reflect that all those words will be branded in my memory, and eating deeper eternally after you have left me? You know you lie to say I have killed you: and, Catherine, you know that I could as soon forget you as my existence! Is it not sufficient for your infernal selfishness, that while you are at peace I shall writhe in the torments of hell?"

"I shall not be at peace," moaned Catherine, recalled to a sense of physical weakness by the violent, unequal throbbing of her heart, which beat visibly and audibly under this excess of agitation. She said nothing further till the paroxysm was over; then she continued, more kindly—

"I'm not wishing you greater torment than I have, Heathcliff. I only wish us never to be parted: and should a word of mine distress you hereafter, think I feel the same distress underground, and for my own sake, forgive me! Come here and kneel down again! You never harmed me in your life. Nay, if you nurse anger, that will be worse to re-

member than my harsh words! Won't you come here again? Do!"

Heathcliff went to the back of her chair, and leant over, but not so far as to let her see his face, which was livid with emotion. She bent round to look at him; he would not permit it: turning abruptly, he walked to the fireplace, where he stood, silent, with his back towards us. Mrs. Linton's glance followed him suspiciously: every movement woke a new sentiment in her. After a pause and a prolonged gaze, she resumed; addressing me in accents of indignant disappointment:—

"Oh, you see, Nelly, he would not relent a moment to keep me out of the grave. *that* is how I'm loved! Well, never mind. That is not *my* Heathcliff. I shall love mine yet; and take him with me: he's in my soul. And," added she musingly, "the thing that irks me most is this shattered prison, after all. **I'm tired of being enclosed here. I'm wearying to escape into that glorious world, and to be always there: not seeing it dimly through tears, and yearning for it through the walls of an aching heart: but really with it, and in it.** Nelly, you think you are better and more fortunate than I; in full health and strength: you are sorry for me—very soon that will be altered. I shall be sorry for *you*. I shall be incomparably beyond and above you all. I *wonder* he won't be near me!" She went on to herself. "I thought he wished it. Heathcliff, dear! you should not be sullen now. **Do come to me, Heathcliff.**"

Now let's piece the sections in bold together.

"You and Edgar have broken my heart, Heathcliff! And you both come to bewail the deed to me, as if *you* were the people to be pitied! I shall not pity you, not I. You have killed me—and thriven on it, I think. How strong you are! How many years do you mean to live after I am gone?

"I wish I could hold you till we were both dead! I shouldn't care what you suffered. I care nothing for your sufferings. Why shouldn't you suffer? I do! Will you forget me? Will you be happy when I am in the earth?

"I'm not wishing you greater torment than I have, Heathcliff. I only wish us never to be parted: and should a word of mine distress you hereafter, think I feel the same

distress underground, and for my own sake, forgive me! Come here and kneel down again! You never harmed me in your life. Nay, if you nurse anger, that will be worse to remember than my harsh words.

"I'm tired of being enclosed here. I'm wearying to escape into that glorious world, and to be always there: not seeing it dimly through tears, and yearning for it through the walls of an aching heart: but really with it, and in it. Do come to me, Heathcliff."

You can see that by eliminating the dialogue, other characters, and narrative and descriptive phrases, we have created a more compelling monologue.

Now here are two examples of how to create a monologue from a scene in a play. The first play is *The Taming of the Shrew* by William Shakespeare. This scene is between two servants, Grumio and Curtis.

> GRUMIO Fie, fie on all tired jades, on all mad masters, and all foul ways! Was ever man so beaten? Was ever man so rayed? Was ever man so weary? I am sent before to make a fire, and they are coming after to warm them. Now, were not I a little pot and soon hot, my very lips might freeze to my teeth, my tongue to the roof of my mouth, my heart in my belly, ere I should come by a fire to thaw me: but I, with blowing the fire, shall warm myself; for, considering the weather, a taller man than I will take cold. Holla, ho! Curtis.
>
> *Enter CURTIS.*

CURTIS Who is that calls so coldly?

GRUMIO A piece of ice: if thou doubt it, thou mayst slide from my shoulder to my heel with no greater a run but my head and my neck. A fire, good Curtis.

CURTIS Is my master and his wife coming, Grumio?

GRUMIO O, ay, Curtis, ay: and therefore fire, fire; cast on no water.

CURTIS Is she so hot a shrew as she's reported?

GRUMIO She was, good Curtis, before this frost: but, thou knowest, winter tames man, woman and beast; for it hath tamed my old master and my new mistress and myself, fellow Curtis.

CURTIS Away, you three-inch fool! I am no beast.

GRUMIO Am I but three inches? why, thy horn is a foot; and so long am I at the least. But wilt thou make a fire, or shall I complain on thee to our mistress, whose hand, she being now at hand, thou shalt soon feel, to thy cold comfort, for being slow in thy hot office?

CURTIS I prithee, good Grumio, tell me, how goes the world?

GRUMIO A cold world, Curtis, in every office but thine; and therefore fire: do thy duty, and have thy duty; for my master and mistress are almost frozen to death.

CURTIS There's fire ready; and therefore, good Grumio, the news.

GRUMIO Why, "Jack, boy! ho! boy!" and as much news as will thaw.

CURTIS Come, you are so full of cony-catching!

GRUMIO Why, therefore fire; for I have caught extreme cold. Where's the cook? is supper ready, the house trimmed, rushes strewed, cobwebs swept; the serving-men in their new fustian, their white stockings, and every officer his wedding-garment on? Be the jacks fair within, the jills fair without, the carpets laid, and every thing in order?

CURTIS All ready; and therefore, I pray thee, news.

GRUMIO First, know, **my horse is tired; my master and mistress fallen out.**

CURTIS How?

GRUMIO **Out of their saddles into the dirt; and thereby hangs a tale.**

CURTIS Let's ha't, good Grumio.

GRUMIO Lend thine ear.

CURTIS Here.

GRUMIO There.

Strikes him.

CURTIS This is to feel a tale, not to hear a tale.

GRUMIO And therefore 'tis called a sensible tale: and this
cuff was but to knock at your ear, and beseech listening.
Now I begin: **Imprimis, we came down a foul hill, my
master riding behind my mistress,—**

CURTIS Both of one horse?

GRUMIO What's that to thee?

CURTIS Why, a horse.

GRUMIO Tell thou the tale: but hadst thou not crossed me,
**thou shouldst have heard how her horse fell and she
under her horse; thou shouldst have heard in how
miry a place, how she was bemoiled, how he left her
with the horse upon her, how he beat me because her
horse stumbled, how she waded through the dirt to
pluck him off me, how he swore, how she prayed, that
never prayed before, how I cried, how the horses ran
away, how her bridle was burst, how I lost my crupper,
with many things of worthy memory, which now shall
die in oblivion and thou return unexperienced to thy
grave.**

Now here is the monologue pieced together:

GRUMIO **Fie, fie on all tired jades, on all mad masters, and
all foul ways! Was ever man so beaten? Was ever man
so rayed? Was ever man so weary? I am sent before to
make a fire, and they are coming after to warm them.
Now, were not I a little pot and soon hot, my very lips
might freeze to my teeth, my tongue to the roof of my
mouth, my heart in my belly, ere I should come by a
fire to thaw me: but I, with blowing the fire, shall warm
myself; for, considering the weather, a taller man than
I will take cold. My horse is tired; my master and mistress fallen out. Out of their saddles into the dirt; and
thereby hangs a tale. Imprimis, we came down a foul
hill, my master riding behind my mistress,—
Thou shouldst have heard how her horse fell and
she under her horse; thou shouldst have heard in how
miry a place, how she was bemoiled, how he left her
with the horse upon her, how he beat me because her**

horse stumbled, how she waded through the dirt to pluck him off me, how he swore, how she prayed, that never prayed before, how I cried, how the horses ran away, how her bridle was burst, how I lost my crupper, with many things of worthy memory, which now shall die in oblivion and thou return unexperienced to thy grave.

The second monologue is Joan La Pucelle from *Henry VI, Part One* by William Shakespeare. She is speaking to the Dauphin (later the King of France) and other officers in his court.

JOAN LA PUCELLE

Dauphin, I am by birth a shepherd's daughter,
My wit untrain'd in any kind of art.
Heaven and our Lady gracious hath it pleased
To shine on my contemptible estate:
Lo, whilst I waited on my tender lambs,
And to sun's parching heat display'd my cheeks,
God's mother deigned to appear to me
And in a vision full of majesty
Will'd me to leave my base vocation
And free my country from calamity:
Her aid she promised and assured success:
In complete glory she reveal'd herself;
And, whereas I was black and swart before,
With those clear rays which she infused on me
That beauty am I bless'd with which you see.
Ask me what question thou canst possible,
And I will answer unpremeditated:
My courage try by combat, if thou darest,
And thou shalt find that I exceed my sex.
Resolve on this, thou shalt be fortunate,
If thou receive me for thy warlike mate.

CHARLES

Thou hast astonish'd me with thy high terms:
Only this proof I'll of thy valour make,
In single combat thou shalt buckle with me,
And if thou vanquishest, thy words are true;
Otherwise I renounce all confidence.

JOAN LA PUCELLE

> I am prepared: here is my keen-edged sword,
> Deck'd with five flower-de-luces on each side;
> The which at Touraine, in Saint Katharine's churchyard,
> Out of a great deal of old iron I chose forth.

CHARLES

> Then come, o' God's name; I fear no woman.

JOAN LA PUCELLE

> And while I live, I'll ne'er fly from a man.

Here they fight, and JOAN LA PUCELLE overcomes.

CHARLES

> Stay, stay thy hands! thou art an Amazon
> And fightest with the sword of Deborah.

JOAN LA PUCELLE

> Christ's mother helps me, else I were too weak.

CHARLES

> Whoe'er helps thee, 'tis thou that must help me:
> Impatiently I burn with thy desire;
> My heart and hands thou hast at once subdued.
> Excellent Pucelle, if thy name be so,
> Let me thy servant and not sovereign be:
> 'Tis the French Dauphin sueth to thee thus.

JOAN LA PUCELLE

> I must not yield to any rites of love,
> For my profession's sacred from above:
> When I have chased all thy foes from hence,
> Then will I think upon a recompense.

CHARLES

> Meantime look gracious on thy prostrate thrall.

REIGNIER

> My lord, methinks, is very long in talk.

ALENCON

> Doubtless he shrives this woman to her smock;
> Else ne'er could he so long protract his speech.

REIGNIER

> Shall we disturb him, since he keeps no mean?

ALENCON

> He may mean more than we poor men do know:
> These women are shrewd tempters with their tongues.

REIGNIER

    My lord, where are you? what devise you on?

    Shall we give over Orleans, or no?

JOAN LA PUCELLE

    Why, no, I say, distrustful recreants!

    Fight till the last gasp; I will be your guard.

CHARLES

    What she says I'll confirm: we'll fight it out.

JOAN LA PUCELLE

    Assign'd am I to be the English scourge.

    This night the siege assuredly I'll raise:

    Expect Saint Martin's summer, halcyon days,

    Since I have entered into these wars.

    Glory is like a circle in the water,

    Which never ceaseth to enlarge itself

    Till by broad spreading it disperse to nought.

    With Henry's death the English circle ends;

    Dispersed are the glories it included.

    Now am I like that proud insulting ship

    Which Caesar and his fortune bare at once.

Now here is the monologue pieced together. Notice that I have rearranged the order a bit. I have also made the monologue only spoken to the Dauphin. It is too confusing to include multiple characters.

JOAN LA PUCELLE

    Dauphin, I am by birth a shepherd's daughter,

    My wit untrain'd in any kind of art.

    Heaven and our Lady gracious hath it pleased

    To shine on my contemptible estate:

    Lo, whilst I waited on my tender lambs,

    And to sun's parching heat display'd my cheeks,

    God's mother deigned to appear to me

    And in a vision full of majesty

    Will'd me to leave my base vocation

    And free my country from calamity:

    Her aid she promised and assured success:

    In complete glory she reveal'd herself;

And, whereas I was black and swart before,
With those clear rays which she infused on me
That beauty am I bless'd with which you see.
Ask me what question thou canst possible,
And I will answer unpremeditated:
Assign'd am I to be the English scourge.
This night the siege assuredly I'll raise:
Expect Saint Martin's summer, halcyon days,
Since I have entered into these wars.
Glory is like a circle in the water,
Which never ceaseth to enlarge itself
Till by broad spreading it disperse to nought.
With Henry's death the English circle ends;
Dispersed are the glories it included.
Now am I like that proud insulting ship
Which Caesar and his fortune bare at once.
My courage try by combat, if thou darest,
And thou shalt find that I exceed my sex.
Resolve on this, thou shalt be fortunate,
If thou receive me for thy warlike mate.

Make the Circumstances Clear

If you're writing your own monologues, creating your own monologues from other sources, or piecing together speeches from a dialogue scene in a play, you want to make the monologue self-explanatory. Don't refer to a character that the auditor won't recognize. Even if it's a well-known play, don't assume that that auditor has seen it. There are some people in this business who have very little background in theater, especially in Los Angeles because the industry there is focused on television and films. Make the circumstances crystal clear immediately. Don't wait until you're two-thirds of the way through the monologue to do that. Give the auditors the information they need to know right at the beginning. Set up the situation, because, if you don't, they're going to be sitting there wondering, "Well, who is George?" And then they're not giving you their full attention. Instead, they're focused on trying to figure out what is going on.

Create a Conflict

When you create a monologue from another source, such as a book, make sure there's a conflict in it. It shouldn't be just straight narrative or beautiful writing that's very descriptive. Many fiction writers make very poor playwrights, because they tend to be too flowery and the writing is not active enough.

Above all else, make sure your monologue is active. Often reporters make the best writers, because they pare things down to the facts, and they leave the conclusions to the reader, or, in our case, the audience. This is good because it keeps the audience involved. You want something that really packs a punch. Action and conflict are the things that pack a punch on stage.

Summary

Rules for editing and piecing material into a monologue.

1. Hit the high points.
2. Make sure the circumstances are self-explanatory.
3. There must be a conflict.

CHAPTER FOUR

Audition Preparation

Rehearsal Techniques

At this point in the process, you should have a monologue that is little known. It fits you because you've done research on who you are and what qualities you want to market. You have also edited and shaped it, so it has a beginning, a middle, an end, and a conflict. Now you have to get your piece up on its feet and ready to go.

Working with a Partner

Many actors find it difficult to rehearse monologues on their own. It's hard just standing there talking to a wall. Actors need audiences. In working with actors, I found that many of them had an easier time doing monologues from plays in which they had actually appeared. This is because they could remember the reactions of the other actors in the play. They carried those memories to the audition and reacted to them all over again. If you have a friend who will work with you, you can recreate those conditions again by doing the following exercise.

EXERCISE

Find a friend who will listen to your monologue. Have your friend talk back to you and make the monologue into a scene. Ask your friend to oppose what you want in the monologue. For example, if your objective is to get someone's help, have your partner refuse to give it to you. This makes for conflict. Conflict holds the auditor's attention.

Creating a Character History

When you get a new monologue, you should first read the play it came from, and take notes on your character. See what the character says about himself or herself and what other people say about him or her. Then create the character's history. Even if the playwright doesn't give you any information, you must figure out the character's background.

Many actors don't want to do this. They say "Can't I just do the monologue? Do I have to read the play?"

It's for your own benefit to do this work. Then you're not showing up at the audition as yourself with your problems and your nervousness. You're coming to the audition as this imaginary person in the middle of a life that you've created. You're coming from some place, going to some place. And in the middle of all of that, you do this monologue in which you're trying to get something you want from somebody else. If you really know this character's life very intimately, it will take the focus off your anxieties about yourself at the audition. It will also give you ideas that you may not have thought of about how to do your monologue and what your character is like.

You'll know who this person is and what he or she would do in any situation. So nothing can throw you at the audition.

Answer the following questions about your character. You can actually write out the answers, or if you prefer, just think about them. I suggest recording the questions. Then lie down, close your eyes, and imagine the answers. You may choose to use some of the information provided by the playwright. Or you can do the monologue out of context and create a new history for the character. If you choose to do this, be careful. Some monologues are very generic and will work for many different types of actors. Others are too specific to be done out of context. For example, if you are a real New York type, don't do a monologue from *Of Mice and Men*, which is specifically written about characters on a ranch. If you try to change its setting to New York, the writing won't support that choice, and you run the risk of confusing the auditors.

Character History Questions

1. Where are you from?
2. What is your occupation?
3. What is your economic status?
4. What is your religion?
5. What are your politics?
6. What is your sexual orientation?
7. What is your education level?
8. What is your IQ?
9. What is your immediate goal?
10. What are your long-range goals?
11. Do you drink or smoke?
12. Do you have any hobbies?
13. What are your prejudices, if any?
14. Do you have any bad habits?
15. What is your favorite food, drink, movie, TV show?
16. What is the nicest thing you ever did?
17. What is the meanest thing you ever did?
18. What are you most afraid of?
19. Describe the happiest day of your life.

20. Describe the saddest day of your life.

21. Did you get along with you parents/siblings?

22. As a child, who were you closest to in your family?

23. Who are you close to now?

24. When you enter a room, do you take center stage or fade into the woodwork?

25. How do you dress?

26. What is your body like?

27. What is the leading center of energy in your body?

28. What do you think of Marx, Warhol, Brad Pitt, Shakespeare, Gloria Steinem, Tennessee Williams, Barack Obama, Jane Austen?

29. What is the best present you ever received?

30. Are you a day or night person?

31. Who do you look up to?

32. Who do you hate?

33. Are you an indoor or an outdoor person?

34. Do you drive? If so, what kind of car?

35. Describe your friends.

36. What do you do for fun?

37. Describe your living space.

38. What kind of perfume do you wear, if any?

39. Do you have any physical problems—illnesses, ailments?

40. Describe yourself in a word or phrase (for example, martyr, bully).

41. Are you musical?

42. What kind of music do you like?

43. What sports do you like or do, if any?

44. Do you have any secrets?

45. Do you like to dance? What kind of dancing do you like?

46. What are your most positive and negative traits?

47. Do you have any children? How do you feel about children?

48. Do you have any pets?

49. What is your favorite animal?

50. If you were an animal, which one would you be?

51. Describe your sexual history.

52. How do you treat people who have more or less power than you do?

53. Are you successful?

54. Describe your attitude towards life in a sentence, for example, "Life is a struggle," or "Life is just a bowl of cherries."

55. What newspaper do you read?

56. How do you wear your hair?

57. What's your favorite flower?

58. What are your superstitions?

59. Are you interested in the occult?

60. Do you have any addictions?

61. What are the major events in your life that have made you the person you are today (for example, the death of a parent, molestation, loss of money)?

62. What historical figure would you like to meet?

63. What possession would you save in a fire?

64. What does your character think of you?

65. Did you do well in school?

66. What do you think of designer clothes, pornography, racism, the arts, technological age, death, crime, money?

67. Have you had a hard or easy life?

68. Are you sophisticated?

69. Describe your sense of humor (for example, sarcastic, wry).

Life Improvisations

Since you often have no partner to rehearse with when you work on your monologue, a great rehearsal technique for working on monologues is "Life Improvisations." These exercises give you ideas for your character that a director would probably never think of. They come right out of your imagination. They also help you discover the character's physicality. You will learn his or her rhythm, posture, and how the character moves.

EXERCISE

Get up in the morning and become your character. Eat what the person eats for breakfast, and wear what he or she wears. Then go out and walk around as the character. Take your character to a store and see what he or she buys. Or you might make a phone call to someone as your character. Don't call someone you know. That person might not understand. Instead, call a stranger like the operator at the bus terminal or the airlines. Take your character some place where he or she would be uncomfortable. You could also take your character to a public place like a restaurant. See how your character interacts with the waiter. You will learn so much about your character by getting on your feet and becoming him or her.

EXERCISE

Once you have finished your life improvisations, there are other improvisations you can do that can be very freeing.

1. Do your monologue in gibberish or baby talk.
2. Rehearse your monologue silently, doing the physical movements and just thinking the lines.
3. Paraphrase the monologue in your own words.
4. Rehearse your monologue, expanding on the lines. Use the lines of the piece and your own words in between each line.

5. Do the whole monologue jumping up and down.

6. Do the whole monologue pushing against the wall.

7. Do a completely crazy version of your monologue. Make a fool of yourself.

8. Do the monologue while performing a physical activity such as bouncing a ball or riding a bicycle.

Collecting Objects

EXERCISE

Collect objects that your character might have. Cut pictures out of magazines or use old photographs and make a scrapbook for your character. All this work will help you to understand who your character is in a very specific, concrete way.

Memorization and Staging

There are several different ways of memorizing. Some people like to drill the monologue into their heads right away and get it out of the way. Other people feel that that's too mechanical. They like to rehearse with the script in their hands, and eventually, the lines just sink in. Others record their monologue and listen to it over and over. Some actors make a list of the main ideas the character talks about and memorize that way. Others will improvise around the lines and gradually eliminate their own lines until only the written text remains. Marlon Brando didn't like to memorize lines because he said it interfered with the spontaneity of the moment. So he taped cards with his lines just out of camera range and read them. Of course, you can't do this in a play.

If you are Marlon Brando, you can get away with this on a movie set, but the average actor may run into problems trying this technique.

It doesn't matter how you learn your monologue as long as you learn it. Your goal is to know your monologue so well that you don't even have to think of the lines. They're second nature.

If you get to the audition and forget the words, just make something up. Never stop and tell the auditors that you don't know the line. Nine times out of ten, they're not going to know your monologue word for word, unless you do something that they've heard a million times, and even then you should still try to fake it. Be prepared. Showing off your acting skills is infinitely more important then showing the auditors how perfectly you've memorized your piece. That's where the homework comes in. If you really know this character well, you can improvise to get yourself back on track. But if you've just learned the monologue the night before, which I don't advocate, it's going be harder.

I have gotten phone calls from actors who tell me, "This agent wants me to come back tomorrow and do a monologue. Can you get me something today? I memorize really fast."

I say to that person, "Yes, but it's not just about memorizing. It's about really becoming this character, knowing who this person is, and letting it settle in. It's difficult to do this in a day."

Keeping in Shape

I often tell actors to go to every audition they can, so that they can stay in shape. It's especially helpful to go to auditions that you don't care about because you will learn a lot from them. When the pressure's off, you can really experiment and have fun with your piece. Then you'll be much more ready for the big audition when it comes along. If you wait till the night before to learn something, you're putting tremendous pressure on yourself. It's much more likely that you're going to have a problem when you get there because you're only human. Nerves kick in. There are distractions in the room, sometimes outside the room. The auditors could be eating their lunch during your monologue, or the heater could suddenly come on, and you might have to start speaking much louder. If you're easily distracted, it's going to throw you. Get in the habit of practicing these rehearsal techniques daily or at least several times a week. Make them part of your daily routine, and you will start to see results.

Stage Versus Film Monologues

Practice your monologue two ways. First do it in a very intimate way, as if you're talking to the camera. Then practice a bigger version, as if you're trying to fill a theater or talking to a large group.

You should have an office version and a stage version. In the office version, you sit in a chair and don't move around too much. You might get out of the chair, if there's room. But you shouldn't do much more than that.

However, if you're on the stage of a theater or in a large space, you should do more. The auditors want to see you move. So be prepared. You can do your homework in regard to this. Find out where the audition is and what kind of space it's going to be in. Knowing this can be very helpful in planning how you're going to do your piece.

Beginnings and Endings

Practice every phase of your audition, from the moment you enter the room to the moment you leave. You should rehearse entering the room, saying your name, and announcing your pieces. You should also practice going from one monologue to another. Finally, you should end your piece in a definite way. Don't just stand there and say, "Scene." Walk upstage, or collapse in a chair, or do something very definite to let the auditors know that the monologue is over.

If they ask you any questions, answer in a friendly and concise way. If they give you directions and ask you to do your piece a different way, try it without any argument. Many auditors want to make sure that you are cooperative and can take direction. They want to hire an actor who will be easy to work with. If you give a great audition but seem difficult, you may not get the job. When the audition is over, thank the auditors and leave. Do not try to engage them in conversation or ask for feedback. They don't have time for that.

Doing these rehearsals consistently with your monologues will greatly improve your auditions.

Summary

1. Rehearse with a partner.
2. Create a character history.
3. Do "life improvisations" and other improvisations to free yourself.
4. Collect objects for your character.
5. Memorize and block your piece.
6. Go to as many auditions as possible to stay in shape.
7. Rehearse a stage and film version of your monologue.
8. Practice beginning and ending the piece and entering and leaving the room.

CHAPTER FIVE

Script Analysis

Emotional Preparation

Before you begin the monologue, you will need to do an emotional preparation to create the emotional state that the character is experiencing. Don't just go into the audition and hope you are in the mood that day. You've got to do your homework. A dancer goes to the bar and does fifty plies a day, and a pianist practices scales before playing a concerto. You need to practice your emotional preparation.

Many great actors do daily emotional recall exercises so that their emotions are very much at their fingertips. If the first line of a monologue calls for them to burst into tears, they know how to push their own buttons and make that happen. That should be your goal, because if you can't do that, the next person coming in after you may do it very well. And that person will have an edge over you.

To do an emotional preparation, first, you must examine the text and figure out what your character's state of mind is right before the monologue begins. If you don't know, you have to make it up based on whatever information you can get from the piece. If you don't have the complete script, then you have to use your imagination. When you are figuring out your character's emotional state right before your piece begins, try to describe his or her feelings very simply. For example, the character is angry, fearful, or sad. Avoid going into some convoluted description such as "He wishes he had made a different choice, but he didn't, so now he doesn't know what to do." That gets you into your head too much, and it's hard to act. So keep it simple, and whatever you do, make a strong choice. After you decide what emotion your character is feeling, there are numerous ways to go about getting yourself into that emotional state.

Emotional Recall Techniques

THE STANISLAVSKY METHOD

The Stanislavsky Method recommends using events from your own life to get yourself into a particular emotional state.

EXERCISE

To practice this technique, let's imagine you have a monologue in which you learn that your father has just died. You have to burst into tears on your first line.

1. Remember when your father or someone you were close to died, and relive that incident in great detail. Start with the moment when you got the news. Where were you? Who was there? What did you say? What did you do?

2. If no one in your life has died, think of a time when you experienced a loss. Maybe there was a time when your boyfriend broke up with you. Perhaps your best friend moved away when you were a child, or maybe you lost your most precious possession. Relive one of these events in your mind in great detail.

3. If you can't think of a loss in your life, just remember any time you felt really sad and relive that incident.

It doesn't matter what you use. The auditors will never know what you use. Anything that makes you very, very sad and upset will work.

THE MEISNER TECHNIQUE

The Meisner Technique, created by the well-known acting teacher Sanford Meisner, takes a different approach. This technique does not advocate using events from your life to do an emotional preparation. Meisner teachers say, "Use your imagination." Make up a scene that could have happened in your own life, or imagine yourself in the character's situation in the play.

EXERCISE

Let's take as an example the monologue about getting the news of your father's death. According to the Meisner Technique you can get in the mood by using your imagination.

Imagine your father lying in a coffin. Imagine your mother crying. Imagine going up and touching his hands. Feel how hard and cold they are. Dwell on the details of this imagined scene, and make them seem very real to yourself.

We do this all the time in real life. We imagine things are going to happen that never do. For example, when you're a teenager about to go out on your first date, you dream about how wonderful it will be in great detail. Or maybe you have a lump on your leg. You imagine it's cancer and play out the amputation in your mind. Good actors are imaginative people. Doing emotional preparation is just fantasizing in a more conscious way.

UTA HAGEN'S SENSORY OBJECTS

Uta Hagen, the acclaimed actor and acting teacher, advocates another technique. It involves using objects from your own life experiences.

EXERCISE

Collect objects from an incident that was upsetting to you. You don't have to literally collect them, although if you have an object that has a very strong emotional charge for you, that can be very helpful. But if not, the exercise will still work. Imagine that you have your meaningful object in your hand. Then relax, take a few deep breaths, and imagine you're touching the object.

We will use the example of the monologue about your father's death again. If your father is dead in real life, remember certain objects from the time when you found out about his death. Describe the room you were in when you got the news. Remember the couch, the chairs, the floor, the phone. Now choose one of these objects and imagine you're touching it. For example, you could choose the phone. Actually reach out and feel it.

And as you do that, free-associate through your five senses.

Notice if you smell anything. Maybe you smell the lilies at the church. Keep touching your object. Notice if you see anything. You might see your father's face. Do you hear anything? Perhaps you hear the organ playing a hymn. Continue touching your object. Notice its texture. It could be smooth and cold. Do you taste anything? Maybe you taste the ham sandwich you had after the funeral.

After you've done all this, emotion should start bubbling up. If not, pick another object and go through the same exercise. If you haven't experienced any deaths in your life, then remember a loss you've had. Think of objects from that incident, and go through this same process with them.

This is a good way to tap into your emotions without working on them directly. Some actors feel that when they use the Stanislavsky Method, they tend to push the emotion. Or they keep checking themselves to see if they are feeling the proper emotion. This technique takes the pressure off because you are just free-associating and seeing what happens.

Our senses often provide powerful links to our emotions. French writer Marcel Proust wrote a series of classic novels collectively called *Remembrance of Things Past*. In the first book, the narrator goes into a bakery and smells some cookies called "Madeleines." This causes emotional memories from his childhood to come flooding back.

Many great actors, such as Geraldine Page, have practiced this technique daily, so that their emotions are very accessible. If they need them, they just need to think of their object, and they can turn on their emotions like a light switch. So, practice, practice, practice!

MUSIC

Another emotional preparation technique is using music to get yourself into a particular emotional state. The actor James Dean was very good at this. He had certain songs that would make him feel upset. Maybe you have a song that reminds you of a broken romance or of a happy time in your life. Get a CD of it, and play it when you need to be in that emotional state. I have seen actors sitting at auditions with headphones on, conjuring up their emotional state. Headphones are a good idea at auditions even if you don't listen to anything. They tend to make other people leave you alone. And that's what you want at auditions. You don't want to engage in a lot of conversations because it's very distracting. You should try to focus on your character and what that character wants and not get into conversations that might pull you out of that reality.

THE PSYCHOLOGICAL GESTURE

There's another technique for emotional preparation that was developed by an acting teacher named Michael Chekhov. It's called "The Psychological Gesture." Chekhov's theory is that if you do a physical activity associated with an emotion over and over, the emotion will follow. For example, if when you are angry, you always pound on the wall or a pillow, then, Chekhov says, you should start pounding and you will get angry. Some people feel this is working from the outside in, but it can be a very effective way to get in touch with emotions.

Crying on Cue

When I was in drama school, there was a lot of emphasis placed on being able to cry on cue. The faculty even gave an award called the "Golden Onion" to the best spontaneous crier. All the students were very competitive over this award. One student even went so far as to gag herself or pull out nasal hairs before every scene that required tears. It makes your eyes water. The teachers never found out her secret.

I don't advocate doing that. I think that there is much too much emphasis placed on the ability to cry. If you can do it, it doesn't necessarily mean you're a good actor. In fact, the woman who won the Golden Onion in my drama school quit acting and became a professional wrestler.

It is important to get yourself in the appropriate emotional state before your monologue, but you don't always have to be weeping buckets. As someone once said, "When you cry, the audience doesn't."

Experiment with these techniques. See what works for you.

Where Are You?

Next, you should know where this monologue is taking place. Make it some place that you know, a place that triggers strong feelings in you. Picture where the furniture is in the room and what's on the fourth wall, which is the invisible wall between you and the audience.

Knowing the setting of your monologue helps to ground you and give you more reality about the circumstances.

Style

When studying your monologue, try to determine the style of the piece. It helps if you can read the play, or if you are familiar with other works by the playwright. If you don't know anything about the original source, often the language and the references will give you a clue. In period pieces, you will immediately notice that the characters speak very differently from the way we speak today. Keep this in mind, and make sure your speech and movement are in keeping with the period in which the play was written.

If you are doing Shakespeare, go through and underline the words which should be stressed. This will actually help you to act. As the famous British theater director Margaret Webster once said, "In Shakespeare, the words are the action."

When Stanislavsky rehearsed Shakespeare's plays with his company, they frequently spent time figuring out the correct stress in the speeches. Many American actors resist doing this. They say they just want to "feel it." Unfortunately, this resistance means that many of them cannot be understood.

The British often go to the other extreme. They are very technically proficient when it comes to doing Shakespeare. After all, they get it with the mother's milk. But many times, they haven't done the emotional work to make their acting really moving. You must have a great technique as well as an emotional connection to your material.

Also, in doing the classics, make sure your physical movements aren't too contemporary. In general, don't use a lot of hand gestures. People in previous centuries tended to move with more decorum and restraint than we do today.

Doing a classic play is not the only time you should pay attention to the style of a piece. I have often seen actors mistake a comedy for a serious play and vice versa. This can be a disaster at an audition, especially if the play is well known.

Certain contemporary playwrights have a very distinctive style. If you are doing a monologue by Tennessee Williams, make sure you use the poetry in his writing to inform your character choices. If you are doing a monologue by Christopher Durang, be aware that his style is a bit over the top. The characters are not always totally realistic. They are frequently larger than life.

High Stakes

Once you have a clear picture of the style of your monologue and the place in which it occurs, then you have to figure out how to infuse your monologue with high stakes. Every monologue and every scene should be a matter of life and death.

Give yourself a reason why you have to get what you want in the next five minutes and make up some dire consequences if you don't get it. This can even work in comedies. If this scenario doesn't work for you, substitute a situation from your life in which you were desperate to change someone's mind.

Identifying the Conflict

You also have to know what the conflict is. What do you want as opposed to what the other character wants? There should be conflict in every scene or monologue.

Sometimes if you have a monologue that tells a story, it's hard to find the conflict. It's really not in the writing. Many actors prefer those monologues where the conflict is very apparent in the writing. However, you can still identify the conflict in a monologue that tells a story. You just have to be more of a detective. In the following monologue from *Ivanov* by Anton Chekhov, Ivanov is telling his problems to his friend. It may seem like he is just telling a story about his troubles, but if you read the script, you can see that he actually wants his friend's help.

> IVANOV I used to have a workman called Simon, you re-
> member him. Once, at threshing time, to show the girls
> how strong he was, he loaded himself with two sacks
> of rye, and broke his back. He died soon after. I think I
> have broken my back also. First I went to school, then

to the university, then came the cares of this estate, all my plans—I did not believe what others did; did not marry as others did; I worked passionately, risked everything; no one else, as you know, threw their money away to right and left as I did. So I heaped the burdens on my back, and it broke. We are all heroes at twenty, ready to attack anything, to do everything, and at thirty are worn-out, useless men. Only a man equally miserable and suffering, as Paul is, could love or esteem me now. Good God! How I loathe myself! How bitterly I hate my voice, my hands, my thoughts, these clothes, each step I take! How ridiculous it is, how disgusting! Less than a year ago I was healthy and strong, full of pride and energy and enthusiasm. I worked with these hands here, and my words could move the dullest man to tears. I could weep with sorrow, and grow indignant at the sight of wrong. I could feel the glow of inspiration, and understand the beauty and romance of the silent nights which I used to watch through from evening until dawn, sitting at my work-table, and giving my soul up to dreams. I believed in a bright future then, and looked into it as trustfully as a child looks into its mother's eyes. And now . . . oh, I am tired and without hope; I spend my days and nights in idleness; I have no control over my feet and brain. My estate is ruined, my woods are falling under the blows of the axe. And what can I think of my treatment of Sarah? I promised her love and happiness forever.

 I opened her eyes to the promise of a future such as she had never dreamed of. She believed me, and though for five years I have seen her sinking under the weight of her sacrifices to me, and losing her strength in her struggles with her conscience, God knows she has never given me one angry look, or uttered one word of reproach. What is the result? That I don't love her! She is suffering; her days are numbered; yet I fly like a contemptible coward from her white face, her sunken chest, her pleading eyes. What is the matter with me? I can't understand it. The easiest way out would be a bullet through the head!

It would be easy to fall into the trap of just complaining. But if Ivanov desperately wants his friend to fix things for him, that adds urgency to that monologue. If you read the play, you will see that this character is in great turmoil.

Perhaps you are given a monologue for an audition and nothing else. If you can't get the play, just use your imagination and make up a scenario in which this monologue might occur.

EXERCISE

Let's practice this technique on the following monologue from *Spoon River Anthology* by Edgar Lee Masters.

> MRS. BENJAMIN PANTIER I know that he told that I
>   snared his soul
>   With a snare which bled him to death.
>   And all the men loved him,
>   And most of the women pitied him.
>   But suppose you are really a lady, and have
>   delicate tastes,
>   And loathe the smell of whiskey and onions.
>   And the rhythm of Wordsworth's "Ode" runs in
>   your ears,
>   While he goes about from morning till night
>   Repeating bits of that common thing;
>   "Oh, why should the spirit of mortal be proud?"
>   And then, suppose:
>   You are a woman well endowed,
>   And the only man with whom the law and
>   morality
>   Permit you to have the marital relation
>   Is the very man that fills you with disgust
>   Every time you think of it—while you think of it
>   Every time you see him?
>   That's why I drove him away from home

> **To live with his dog in a dingy room**
> **Back of his office.**

This monologue comes from a book of poetic monologues portraying the residents of an imaginary town called Spoon River. It is often used in acting classes to teach characterization. First, you must identify the conflict in this monologue; next you need to know whom you are talking to. You might imagine that you are talking to a local resident who is critical of you for separating from your husband. This will create a conflict. You have to change her mind. Try to convince her that you did the right thing and get her on your side. Perhaps she is an important person in the town, and if she disapproves of you, the whole town may turn against you.

Always try to visualize the person you're talking to and imagine why you are saying the monologue to this person. Imagine where you are and what you want from the other person.

Don't count on getting help from the playwright. In plays by Beckett and Ionesco and other avant-garde writers, it's often hard to figure out what your character wants. But that's your job. If you absolutely can't think of anything, just play "I'm right and you're wrong." That will often work if all else fails.

The First Ten Seconds

As I mentioned before, your monologue should have a strong opening. If you don't capture the auditors' attention in the first ten seconds, they might not stay with you for your big moment two-thirds of the way into the monologue. Do something initially to make them sit up and take notice, and then pull back and let the monologue build to a climax. For example, you may choose to say the first line very loudly. You could also decide to physicalize the first moment by pounding your fist on the chair or clapping your hands. Make them pay attention to you. Wake them up!

Relationship

Another important element to consider when you work on your monologue is your relationship to the other character.

> **EXERCISE**
>
> Write down your feelings about that other character. Do you love her? Do you hate her? Do you fear her? How does that person feel about you? How do you know each other? Explore the history of your relationship. If you don't know each other, how did you come together to have this interaction?

What Do You Want?

The single most important thing to figure out in any monologue is what you want from the other character. This is known as your objective. If you find an objective that brings you to life, your monologue will work. If not, it will be deadly dull. Cerebral objectives such as "I want her to know I'm a good person" are nearly impossible to act. Try to keep this simple and very active. Acting is about taking action, not wallowing in emotions. Objectives such as to "change his mind" or "get his help" are examples of very simple objectives, which are easily acted.

Beats

Breaking the monologue into beats is a great way to create variety in your piece. Every time the thought changes, it's a new beat. For example, if your monologue is about getting your brother to loan you $1,000, the beats are the ways that you go about getting it from him. In life, when you want something from someone and he's not giving it to you, you have to try different ways to get it from him. The beats are those different actions you take to get what you want from the other person. That's what makes you look like you have an emotional range. If you simply try one tactic throughout, you will be very boring.

You'll be what they call "a one-note actor."

So, if your monologue is about getting that $1,000 from your brother, your first beat might be to flatter him, "I like you so much. You're such a good brother. What a nice shirt you have on. Could you loan me $1,000?" What if he says no? Then you might try to get some sympathy. "Everything is going wrong for me. I'm about to be evicted. I have no job. My wife's sick." If that doesn't work, you might threaten him. "The door is locked and I have a gun in my pocket. And you're not leaving until you give me the money."

When you use these different tactics, you look like you have a big emotional range. That makes you an exciting actor. It's also very important to use action verbs. Starting below, you will find a whole list of verbs that you can use in your monologues. If you have trouble finding action verbs, please refer to it. You will notice that the verbs I give are very active. I do not include unexciting verbs such as "to explain." I can explain how to get from here to the corner, but it's not a very compelling acting choice.

Action Verbs

To accuse	To belittle	To con
To ambush	To betray	To condescend
To analyze	To blame	To confess
To anger	To brag	To confide
To annoy	To build up	To confront
To apologize	To cajole	To conquer
To appeal	To calm down	To control
To arouse	To celebrate	To convert
To attack	To challenge	To convince
To back off	To charm	To crush
To bait	To coax	To dazzle
To beg	To comfort	To decimate

To defend

To defy

To demand

To destroy

To disarm

To discover

To disgrace

To disgust

To disobey

To dominate

To educate

To enrage

To entertain

To excite

To explode

To figure out

To flatter

To forgive

To get approval

To get attention

To get revenge

To get sympathy

To humiliate

To ignore

To impress

To indict

To indoctrinate

To insist

To inspire

To interrogate

To intimidate

To justify

To kill with kindness

To lament

To lecture

To make him beg

To make him feel guilty

To make someone toe
    the line

To make trouble

To manipulate

To mimic

To mock

To negotiate

To nurture

To open your heart

To persecute

To placate

To plead

To praise

To pressure

To probe

To protect

To protest

To provoke

To punish

To push away

To reason

To recreate

To relive

To rescue

To resist

To rev up

To romance

To scare

To seduce

To sell

To smother

To soothe

To spit it out

To stand your
    ground

To steal

To support

To take a stand

To take center stage

To teach

To tell someone off

To terrorize

To threaten

To titillate

To trap

To treat like a child

To trick

To undermine

To unnerve

To wheedle

To win

To wound

Making the Monologue into a Scene

As I said before, when you rehearse, you should always make your monologue into a scene. It's good to work with a friend and have him or her play the other character in your piece and talk back to you. If there is no other character in the scene, then make up a person that your character might be talking to. Write out a response sheet for your imaginary partner.

EXERCISE

Using the monologue about getting $1,000 from your brother, write down your first action: to flatter. Then write down the other person's reaction. Maybe he looks at you like you're crazy. How does that make you feel? What does that make you want to do? Maybe you want to defend yourself on the next beat. Then try that next. How does the other person react to that? How does that make you feel? What does that make you want to do? These kinds of questions will lead you from beat to beat and make the transitions much easier.

Even if you don't have anybody who will talk back to you, you can still have very productive rehearsals with yourself.

When you are analyzing your script, read it over and over. You will get new information every time and become more identified with the world of your character. The well-known actor Michael Caine has said that he rereads his script hundreds of times and finds new information each time. So do the work, map out how you want to do your monologue, and then go in there and do it as if you were saying those words for the first time. As Pablo Casals once said, "Don't play the notes, play the music."

If you have done your homework, you will have a structure to fall back on. Then, even though you will have your good days and your bad days, your monologue will never fall below a certain level. Do the homework that professional actors do, and you will look like a professional at auditions.

Summary

Analyze your script by taking the following steps:

1. Figure out the character's state of mind, and do an emotional preparation.
2. Find out where the monologue occurs and in what time period.
3. Identify the conflict.
4. Infuse the monologue with high stakes.
5. Grab the auditors' attention in the first ten seconds.
6. Define your relationship to the other character.
7. Name your objective.
8. Break the monologue into beats.
9. Make the monologue into a scene, and write out the responses of the other character.

CHAPTER SIX

Frequently Asked Questions

1. **"How should I dress at the audition? Should I wear a costume that the character I'm playing might wear?"**

Whatever you wear should suggest the character, but only slightly. I've seen actors show up at auditions, especially if it's a period piece, in hoop skirts or suits of armor. To me, that seems too desperate. And it's a turnoff to a lot of casting directors.

Mark Simon, who cast *Ragtime* and *Showboat*, was once casting *The King and I*. He complained that many of the women came in with these hairnets called snoods, which the character of Anna wears in the show. He said, "It's not necessary. I have an imagination."

If you're auditioning for a blue-collar type, don't wear a suit. If the character is a little more upscale, wear something dressy. But don't go to extremes; just suggest the character in your attire.

2. **"I get very nervous before an audition. What can I do?"**

It's important to do relaxation exercises before you go to your audition. Do yoga, deep breathing, or the following exercise.

EXERCISE

(Record the following instructions. Lie down and close your eyes. Play the instructions.)

Visualize yourself in your favorite peaceful place of relaxation. Take ten deep breaths. Relax even more deeply. Start with your toes. Imagine a golden light spreading over your toes and melting them into the floor. Let that light spread over your feet. Feel them melting away. Let the light move up your calves, through your knees, into your thighs. Let both of your legs melt into the floor. Now imagine the light moving up into your pelvis. Feel it melting away tensions in your genitals, your intestines. Feel the light moving into your stomach. Let it melt away. Now the light moves into your chest; feel it relaxing your breathing even more. Let it spread up to your shoulders and melt them away. Feel it flowing down your arms into your hands and fingers. Let go. Now let the light go back up your arms to your throat and lower jaw. Everything just relaxes. Now the light spreads across your face, and any tensions you are holding in the mouth, the cheeks, the forehead melt away. Let the light spread up into your scalp and flow down your spine. Feel each vertebra melt into the floor. Take a few more deep breaths. Enjoy the feeling of being totally relaxed. Enjoy being in your favorite peaceful place. Stay there for a few minutes. When you are ready, start moving your hands and feet. Open your eyes. Slowly sit up.

If you're still nervous when you get to the audition, go into the bathroom and jump up and down and shake the nerves out. Or you can push against a wall to release tension. Do whatever you have to do to relax, because tension tends to murder emotions. Even though your character may be tense, you don't want to be.

I used to be so nervous at auditions that I would have to listen to positive thinking tapes. I would shout affirmations like, "I'm the greatest! I can do it! I'm gonna win today!" These recordings put me in such a confident mood that I went into the audition feeling like I could do anything. Don't shout outside the audition room. Affirm your talent silently there. But you might shout affirmations at home before you leave. Then when you get there, you will know how great you are.

EXERCISE

Here is a list of affirmations. Repeat them at least once a day to start filling your mind with positive thoughts about your monologues and auditions. Write them out. Say them before you leave for the audition. Or record them and listen to them just before the audition.

AFFIRMATIONS

I am highly pleasing to agents and casting people.

My auditions always go well.

I enjoy doing monologues.

I am a great actor.

I always do and say the right thing at auditions.

People enjoy seeing me do my monologues.

I feel relaxed and confident at auditions.

I am grateful for my talent.

I know what I am doing at auditions.

People want to work with me.

I've got what it takes.

Auditions are fun.

My monologue is the perfect vehicle for my talent.

I do my monologue brilliantly with ease and without effort.

Everyone sees that I'm talented.

Nothing can throw me at auditions. I know what I'm doing.

I'm in demand.

I'm hot.

I can easily get what I want at auditions.

If you're still nervous, despite all your relaxation exercises and affirmations, incorporate that nervousness into your character. Find a reason for the character to be nervous. Let it be okay to be nervous. The more you try to deny the nerves and make them go away, the more they're going to persist. So just let them be there, and make them part of what you're doing.

There may be distractions in the room that might throw you, such as a drill press in the street or phones ringing in the middle of your monologue. If you're really concentrating on your character, nothing will distract you. But if your attention is on "Do they like me?" or "What are my hands doing?" these little annoyances can really get in the way of your concentration.

3. "How can I prepare for my audition?"

Try to find out all you can about the auditors. If your audition is set up by an agent, you can ask what he or she knows about the casting director at your audition. If you are called directly, ask questions. "What character am I auditioning for?" "How is that character described?" "Will I be doing a monologue or reading from the script?"

There are also books of interviews with casting directors. In these books, they talk about their backgrounds, likes and dislikes, and their pet peeves. So do your homework and research your auditors.

4. "I do my preparation before I go into the room, but I lose it if I meet a friend in the waiting room or if the auditors engage me in a conversation. What should I do?"

I've already talked about not engaging in lengthy conversations in the waiting room. Wear headphones, even if you're not playing anything. If your preparation involves music, you could be listening to your song.

If you're using an emotional recall preparation in which you're touching an imaginary object, just sit there and do that.

If you meet a friend who wants to talk, ask politely if you could speak to him or her after your audition. The same goes for the auditors. If they start interviewing you before you do your piece, just ask if you can do your monologue first and answer their questions after you've finished. If worse comes to worst and you have to talk before doing your monologue, just put it on the back burner. Maybe you've had the experience of being upset about something, even in tears, and suddenly you run into someone that you want to impress. You don't want them to see you crying. So you talk to them, and after they leave, you go right back to being upset. You can do this at auditions, too.

5. "How should I enter the room?"

When you enter the room, enter like a professional. There are teachers who have actually spent weeks teaching students how to enter a room and stand in front of the auditors looking relaxed until they ask you to begin. It's not that easy. Whatever you do, don't go in apologetically. I saw so much of this kind of behavior when I sat in on my agent's audition night. The way people entered the room either captured our attention or made us uninterested. One actor came in carrying several bags and dropping things. Then his umbrella popped open.

He said, "Oh, excuse me. I just came from my temp job. I'm sorry, I'm sorry. Oh, my picture's all wet. I'm sorry."

It was difficult to take this type of person seriously.

Some of them would be asked to sing, and they would say, "Oh, oh, my tape's not cued up. Let me find it. Oh, no, that's not it. No. Oh, just a minute."

By this time, we were looking at our watches. So be prepared and professional. If you're late, your only excuse, whether or not it's true, is you were at another audition. They liked you so much that they kept you overtime. Don't worry, they're not going to check.

You can actually get together with a friend and practice entering the room and announcing your pieces. This first impression of you is important. Many actors can't even say their names clearly. Often, they don't know the correct name of their monologue or of the person who wrote it. Make sure you know this information cold.

Also, read the play your monologue is from. The auditors may want to discuss it with you. You will not make a good impression if they find out you haven't read it. After you announce your name and the names of your pieces, turn your back to the auditors for a second and get in touch with your emotional preparation once again. When I say a second, I mean this literally. They will not take kindly to your wasting their time spending a long time getting into your piece. In fact, an actor I know once asked for ten minutes to get in the mood and was quickly shown the door.

After you have finished your first monologue, turn your back to the auditors for another couple of seconds, and then turn back and begin your next piece. These little technical details can make or break your audition. So be sure to practice them as well as your monologues.

6. "How can I prepare for interviews?"

You should have a story about every credit on your resume. You should be articulate. When the auditor asks, "How was doing *Oklahoma* at the Barn Dinner Theater in Kentucky?" don't just say, "It was good." Instead, give a response in which they can see your personality. You could tell a little story about doing that show.

For instance, "The theatre was right near Robert Duval's house, and he came to our opening night." Name-dropping is always good. Most people in this business are a little starstruck. But even if you don't name-drop, have a story ready in which you will come alive. Think of stories for everything on your resume, because you never know what they will ask you and you want to be prepared.

EXERCISE

Write out a monologue that answers the familiar question "Tell me about yourself?" or "What have you been up to lately?" You don't have to parrot back your credits. Talk about other interests you have, even things that have nothing to do with show business. Don't mention problems or auditions you didn't get. You could talk about the last show you did, if it was particularly interesting. Be a real person in the interview. Don't just be a robot that's on automatic. Try to come alive in your speech about "Tell me about yourself?" Become familiar with the points you want to get across, but don't memorize it. Practice your interview technique with your friends. Ask them to give you feedback, so that you come across as natural and friendly in your interview.

7. "How can I get an interview? I sent out a hundred pictures and resumes and no one called me."
Many actors have trouble even getting an interview. I suggest sending out fifteen to twenty pictures at a time, and then following up with phone calls in which you try to get an appointment. Now, I know that many agents and casting people say "Don't call us, we'll call you." But that's only to cut down on the number of phone calls they get in the office. If you send out pictures and you don't get a response, you have to call the agent or casting director's office. Otherwise, you have wasted the postage. These pictures and resumes are direct mail. We know statistically that direct mail has a very small percentage of return, unless there's a follow-up. So be brave, pick up that phone.

8. "But I get so nervous when I call agents. What should I say?"
There are classes given and books written on cold-calling techniques. Many times, they're geared to sales people. Actors are sales people, and their product is themselves. If you can't find a class or a book on cold calling, here's a list of possible objections you might get and responses you might say to counter those objections.

Objection	Response
We'll call if we're interested.	I thought you might be interested because (tell them why they should be interested).
Let us know when you're in something.	Tell them what you did most recently, what you will be doing, what kinds of parts you love to do.
What is this in reference to?	I'm calling to schedule an interview. If they hesitate, tell them why they should see you.
He's in a meeting.	Befriend the secretary, create a relationship, find out about the office.
What's your number? He'll call you.	I'm just leaving to go to some auditions. What's a good time to call back?
We're not seeing anybody.	Tell them why they should see you. Ask if they're busy. That's great, a lot of places are slow, that's why I want to work with you. If they're slow, say wouldn't that be a good time to meet new people?
Does he know you?	No, but I've heard good things about him, and he's the one person I want to connect with now that I've finished doing project X.
We know you, we love you.	What are you casting now? How do you see me? What kinds of roles do you see me in?
Why isn't your agent calling?	My agent is great, but she represents many people. It's my responsibility to meet casting people because I take my career seriously.

For example, a call might go like this:

"Hello, I'm John Smith, and I'm calling to schedule an appointment with agent X."

"Have you sent your picture?"

"Yes, I did."

"Well, we're not seeing anyone right now."

"Oh, well, I thought he would like to see me because I'm in this incredible show right now. It got great reviews and I was described as a young Martin Short."

You have to talk yourself up. And if worse comes to worst, and you don't get to talk to the agent, then engage the secretary in a conversation. Find out about him or her. Develop a friendship with the secretary. When you call back, call that secretary by his or her name. The friendlier you are with this person, and the more you two get acquainted, the more likely it is that the next time you call, the secretary will put you through to the agent. You may not always get an appointment, but you are developing a relationship that could be helpful.

You never know, in a year that receptionist could be an agent. It happens all the time. If you get the agent's voice mail, just leave your name and number. Don't say you are an actor. If they don't know who you are, they are more likely to return your call. Also, if you are calling an agent or casting person who is a man, and a man answers the phone, assume it's the agent. Use his name. Many times, they will answer their own phone. But just as often, if they do answer and you ask to speak to them, they will pretend they're not there.

The goal of all of this cold calling is to get an audition or interview. But short of that, your goal is to stay on the horse as long as possible.

9. "I don't know where to look during my monologue. Should I use the auditor or not?"

There are very few auditors who want you to do your monologue directly to them. Most actors like to use them because it's helpful to speak to a real person who will respond. But many casting people say, "No, don't use me, because I want to take notes on you. And I want to observe you. I don't want to have to act with you."

So in that case, I would just look right over their heads. Find a point on the wall over their heads or just to the left or right. Don't turn so far in either direction that they just see your profile. You want them to see your full face and all your wonderful expressions. Don't put a chair in the corner and direct your speech to the chair. You don't need it. If you feel comfortable asking if the auditors would mind being used, you can do that, too. But be prepared for them to say no. If so, then just look right above their heads.

10. "I like to use props in my monologue, but I've been told it's not a good idea. What should I do?"

Many casting people will tell you not to bring props to an audition. I generally agree that props are not usually necessary. If your acting is strong enough, I think you can often overcome the need for props. I know actors really love them, but many times, they're just security blankets. However, there are exceptions. I had one student who did a monologue from *Talking With* about a baton twirler. This actor was a championship baton twirler in real life. In the monologue, there were references to specific baton twirling tricks that the character was supposed to demonstrate. Unfortunately, someone had told her never take props to an audition. So when she came to the lines where she was supposed to throw the baton, she simply mimed the tricks. It was so distracting. I advised her to bring her baton and do her tricks, but she wouldn't, because she was faithfully following the rule someone had told her. So you can see that there are certain occasions where a prop would help the monologue. But never use one if it makes a mess. Don't tear up paper and make confetti all over the room, so that you have to spend ten minutes cleaning up afterwards. I've seen people spray soda bottles or make sandwiches during their monologue. Usually it's not necessary, so use a little common sense.

11. "How many monologues do I need?"

Usually, you are asked to do two contrasting contemporary monologues. By contrasting, they usually mean one serious and one comedic, not two very different characters. After you get those together, you need a serious and comedic classical monologue.

I advise doing Shakespeare, because sometimes they specifically ask for a Shakespearean monologue. If you've learned a Molière or Ben Johnson monologue, then you've got to learn another one. It's best to learn one in verse because sometimes you will be asked for that kind of monologue. If you're good at certain kinds of characters that are pretty specific, such as a Southern belle or a homeless man, have those kinds of monologues in your back pocket. But don't do them at every audition. They are too specific for general purposes and will put you in a very small box.

However, I knew this actor who did have only one monologue, and she would do it many different ways. Her monologue was the psychiatrist from *Agnes of God*. She went to an audition one time and did that monologue.

The auditors said, "Well, that's very nice, dear. But the character you're auditioning for is a prostitute. Do you have something else?"

She said, "Just a minute." Then she turned back, and she did the psychiatrist monologue as a prostitute.

The auditors looked at her and said, "What's that from?" They didn't realize that they'd just heard it.

She said, "That was *Agnes of God*."

They said, "Well, that's not the play."

And she said, "Well, I wasn't showing you the play. I was showing you my work."

Unfortunately, she didn't get the job. Maybe some people would be very impressed with the versatility of an actor who could do a monologue many different ways, or with different accents. But you'll probably make your job easier if the writing supports who the character is.

12. "Is it wrong to do a monologue with a dialect?"

I wouldn't recommend doing an accent unless you are audition-ing for a play written in that dialect. Most times, it's too limiting. If you have an accent and haven't lost it, then you have to do a monologue that is in your dialect or one that would work in your dialect. Some famous actors have never lost their accents, for instance, Sissy Spacek, Al Pacino, and Rosie Perez. They have all made their accents work for them. But they are in the minor-ity. If you have an accent, try to lose it. It is important to be able to do as many different kinds of roles as possible if you want to work. An accent limits the number of roles you can play. You can get audio recordings that will teach you how to lose your accent. You can also get ones that teach you how to do different dialects. I urge you to master as many dialects as you can because it makes it possible for you to audition for more roles. Often the auditors may say that even though their play is written in a dialect, you don't have to do it at the audition. I think you should, no matter what they say. It helps them to see you in the role.

If some other actor does the accent and you don't, and you both do great auditions, that actor will have an advantage over you. He or she will most likely get the part if you are both equally good.

If there is a monologue written in a specific dialect that you really want to do, you might try altering it slightly so that it sounds like general American speech. Then you can do it without an accent, and it won't sound strange. For example, if your favor-ite monologue is written in a British dialect, just eliminate words like "bloody" that the average American would not say.

13. "What's the best way to end a monologue and exit the room?"

At the end of your audition, be very professional, thank them and leave. Do not try to engage the auditors in conversation unless they initiate it. Do not ask for feedback. Remember, they are on a tight schedule and usually don't have time for this.

14. "How can I learn from my audition experiences?"

Keep an audition diary. Write down any feedback you might have received. Note how you felt or what somebody might have said to you that day. Also, always keep a record of what you were wearing.

If they call you back, you should wear the same thing. They may remember you as the woman in the purple sweater. So you don't want to confuse them by wearing something different.

All this can go into your audition notebook. You can study it later and really learn from it. It's all part of your market research. I have included an audition diary at the end of this book. I urge you to use it at every audition.

15. "Should I avoid monologues that tell a story?"

I think story monologues can work, but you have to have a really strong need behind them. When my son was a little boy, I used to tell him a story every night. The reason I did that was to put him to sleep. You don't want to have that effect at the audition. You want to wake them up and make them pay attention to you.

When I used to sit in on my agent's audition nights, I was amazed that a majority of the actors who auditioned would just sit in a chair and recite their monologue in a casual way. They had nothing at stake. It was all on one level. My agent would say to me after they left, "I'm not interested in that actor. If they don't care, I don't care."

If you do have a story monologue, be like John Malkovich when he starred on Broadway in *Burn This* in 1987. He had a monologue about somebody taking his parking space. It was a story monologue. He came dashing on stage like he was shot out of a cannon. He was screaming and yelling. Veins were popping out of his head. He was doing a story monologue, but he had such an incredible emotional connection to the material, such commitment, that the audience was on the edge of their seats. They couldn't wait for him to come back on stage. It was a performance they'll never forget.

I urge you to do that. If you're going to do a story monologue, don't just be the narrator, but really connect with it emotionally. Don't fall into the trap that nine out of ten actors fall into and simply narrate the piece.

I know that many actors prefer monologues in which what the character wants is actually in the writing. You may prefer this kind of monologue because you don't have to try and figure out what the character wants.

In spite of this, I still wouldn't rule out story monologues altogether, because I have seen some that are very effective.

16. "Is it better to do a monologue where I am alone on stage rather than ones where I speak to an imaginary person?"

Some of my students have told me that they have had teachers who told them that they should never do a monologue unless they are alone on stage. They cannot be talking to another person. This is a soliloquy. I have not found this to be true, and frankly, I wonder who ever dreamed up this rule. First of all, if you adhere to this rule, you will have a hard time finding monologues because most monologues are spoken to someone else. Secondly, I do not see the benefit in doing such a monologue at all. If you are good actor, you can make a monologue to another person seem real, even if the person is not there.

17. "How should I rehearse my monologue?"

People have asked me if they should practice their monologue in front of a mirror. Many people become very self-conscious acting for the mirror. They start watching themselves instead of concentrating on the monologue. I think doing your piece in the mirror kills your spontaneity. But some people find it helpful.

Also, if you're going to do a monologue from a film, don't watch the movie of somebody else doing it because then you tend to copy that person. You don't want to approach a role with that other performance in mind. Some actors have told me that if they want to watch the movie in which their monologue occurs, they fast-forward through the scene with their monologue in it. Then they don't try to copy the actor who did it.

18. "How long should my monologues be?"

Most monologues are two to three minutes in length. Before you go to the audition, find out what the time limits on your piece are, if any. If none are stated, do a two- to three-minute monologue.

Sometimes you will be asked to do a one-minute, or even a thirty-second monologue. You can either find a monologue of that duration, or you can cut one of your existing monologues down. When you do a very short piece, be sure that it has a beginning, a middle, and an end, and that it is self-explanatory. Even if the piece is short, you don't want to leave the auditors hanging wondering what you are talking about.

19. "Is it wrong to do a monologue with profanity?"

According to a recent article in *The New York Times*, many people have become desensitized to profanity. The article stated that in previous generations four-letter words were a big taboo, while racial slurs were used frequently. Now the opposite seems to be true. If you are auditioning for an older person, you may want to keep this in mind and avoid profanity. However, I think it depends largely on who you are. For example, if you are perfect for a tough guy in a David Mamet play who uses a lot of profanity, you can probably get away with it. If you usually play very Waspy Park Avenue types, then monologues with a great deal of profanity may not be appropriate for you.

If you have a monologue that contains profanity, and you are uncomfortable with it, you can try cutting out those words. A student of mine did that with a monologue from *Spike Heels*. The character was a secretary who really didn't need the four-letter words to get her point across, so eliminating them didn't hurt the piece.

20. "Why do they always ask for monologues at auditions? I prefer doing scenes."

Most actors do prefer doing scenes because they have another person there who will give them a reaction. It is definitely easier than talking to a wall.

When I first came to New York, there seemed to be more re-quests for scenes at auditions. Now the trend is toward doing monologues for a number of reasons.

First, the auditors can focus only on you if you are doing a monologue. If you are doing a scene, sometimes this is more dif-ficult. It's often hard to find a scene that shows off both actors equally well. An actor I know auditioned for The Actors Studio once and was asked to do a scene. The auditors called her partner back and not her. And it wasn't even his audition!

Second, the Equity Principal Interviews, where actors in the Actors' Equity union were interviewed for roles, were eliminated several years ago and replaced by Equity Principal Auditions, in which the actors were asked to do monologues. Many other plac-es that held general auditions followed the example set by Actors' Equity.

But don't despair. If you really prepare your monologue and it fits you like a glove, you have an advantage. Many times, you are given scenes with little time for preparation. Sometimes this can work in your favor, and you will have a great audition. Other times, it may throw you.

Also, the character you are asked to read for may not be right for you. Once at a casting workshop, an agent gave a female stu-dent of mine a scene to read with another actor. She was a qui-et, sweet, rather delicate middle-aged woman. The role she was given was the tough-talking Detective Sipowicz—Dennis Franz's part on *NYPD Blue*.

When she questioned the casting director's choice of material for her, he said "Well, you're about the same age, and I couldn't find anything else. So give it a try."

She did, but the audition didn't go very well. Not only was the character the wrong sex, but also, his personality was the po-lar opposite of hers. If only she'd had the presence of mind to ask to do a monologue instead. Most actors think they are versatile, but they all have their limits. Don't you make that mistake of be-ing talked into reading something that doesn't serve your talents well. Remember, it's your audition. Take charge of it in every way you can so that you will showcase your talents.

21. "Can I play characters of the opposite sex in a monologue?"
Yes, there are some monologues that are written for one particular sex but will work equally well when done by the opposite one. There have been many women who have attempted some of the celebrated male Shakespearean roles, with great success. Nowadays in New York theatre, it is common to see actors in drag. Productions such as *Hairspray* and *Avenue Q* are examples of this trend. However, I do not think you should actually dress as the opposite sex at an audition unless you are auditioning for avant-garde theater or some specific role that requires cross-dressing.

Some monologues will require no adjustments when done by either sex; however, if you refer to things that are specifically associated with one sex, you may have to make some changes to make it work for the opposite one. Often it can be as simple as changing pronouns; other times you may have to change specific references unless you want to make the character gay.

22. "Are there any types of monologues I should avoid?"
I would not do a monologue from a hit Broadway show that is currently running. Many casting people have probably seen it, and they will compare your performance to the actor doing it. Often these comparisons are not favorable to you.

There are some monologues that are so identified with a particular actor that I would advise against doing them. For example, don't do any of Jimmy Stewart's monologues from *Harvey*. That movie is a classic, and it would be very hard to top Stewart's performance.

Other types of monologues to avoid are ones that have very graphic, disgusting descriptions. I am reminded of a monologue about someone that aborted her own baby and then served it to her husband for dinner. I doubt that doing that piece will endear you to the auditors. Also, don't do monologues where you are screaming constantly or threatening the auditors in any way.

Oftentimes, they will associate you with your choice of material and be frightened to work with you.

When I was in high school, I used to go to National Forensic League competitions where we did monologue auditions. One of the favorite monologues done there was one called *The Button*. It was about someone in a padded cell who went insane looking for a missing button from his shirt. At the time, we all thought this monologue was the height of drama. We could scream and yell and roll around the floor. We could really show our acting chops. However, I later found out from one of the auditors that they hated this monologue. They considered it an assault upon them to have to sit there and listen to screaming and yelling for three minutes.

I have even heard casting people advise actors not to do monologues about being an unemployed actor who can't get a job, a waiter, or a temp. They say not to do monologues about being nervous or unprepared at auditions. They feel it sends a negative subliminal message.

23. "Is there any magic formula? What are they looking for in a monologue?"

While there is no magic formula, there are certain general guidelines that do work when doing monologues. I think they want to see who you are in your monologue. They also want to see you come alive and show your emotional range. Whether you make them cry or laugh, you want to evoke an emotional response of some kind from the auditors.

24. "Should I give a description of the circumstances or setting of my monologue before I begin?"

I would advise against this. Remember, they are usually on a tight schedule. Sometimes, such as at the Straw Hat auditions for summer stock, you are even timed. You may be cut off in the middle of your piece if you have wasted your audition time setting the scene for the auditors. As I have said before, your monologue should be self-explanatory. This eliminates the need for lengthy explanations. Add a word or a sentence to the monologue to make the circumstances clear to the auditors, rather than going through a detailed and unnecessary introduction to your piece.

25. "How do I determine the order of my pieces?"

In general, I would do the piece that requires the more difficult emotional preparation first. This way, you can take your time getting yourself in the mood before you enter the room. Then try to do your monologue as soon as you go into the room in order to make sure that you stay connected to your emotional state. If you do the more difficult piece second, you will only have a few seconds to get in touch with your emotions. This can be hard to do. On the other hand, if your first monologue is highly dramatic and at the end of it you are crying hysterically, it could be difficult to instantly switch off the tears and go into a comedy piece. You should experiment and see which order feels most comfortable to you.

26. "What if I'm only allowed to do one monologue? Should it be comedic or dramatic?"

I have heard varying opinions from casting directors on this subject. Some have said that it is depressing to hear one person after another come in and do these highly dramatic monologues in which they scream at the top of their lungs or weep buckets. They say they really appreciate someone who comes in and makes them laugh. Conversely, other casting directors say they can't really see your acting abilities and emotional range in a comedy. They feel dramatic pieces give them a better idea of what you have to offer as an actor. My advice is, if you are only allowed to do one monologue, find out about the project. If it is a comedy, do a comedic monologue. If it is a serious play, do a dramatic one. However, sometimes it is a general audition, and there are no guidelines to go by. In that case, do whichever piece you feel you do best. Some people are natural comedians, like Eddie Murphy; others, like Meryl Streep, are better in dramas. You could also do a seriocomic monologue that combines humorous and dramatic moments. Know your strengths.

27. "How do I stage my piece? Should I follow the stage directions in the script?"

I recommend ignoring the stage directions in the script of a play. They are often written in by a stage manager after the show has been performed for the first time. They are frequently based on the design of the set or blocking of other scenes that are not relevant to your piece. You must create your own blocking based on your experience of the character and the setting in which your audition will take place.

In addition to this, you should avoid miming stage business. I have already discussed not bringing extraneous props to an audition. Also, it is not necessary to mime things such as drinking from a cup or lighting a cigarette. The auditors won't know the script says to do that particular business unless you have a line that refers to it. If you do, I would suggest cutting that line.

Speaking of cigarettes, never smoke at an audition. Don't even ask the auditors' permission. There is a large anti-smoking movement going on in this country right now, and even asking may offend some people. In fact, there are laws in certain states that prohibit smoking on stage. This may be the wave of the future, so don't ruin your audition by getting involved in this controversial issue.

28. "Speaking of controversial issues, what about doing monologues on hot-button topics such as abortion or gay rights?"

If you're uncomfortable talking about these subjects, don't do a monologue about them. However, if you're the type of person who feels passionate about causes, a monologue on one of these subjects may really inspire you. Research your auditors and make your decision based on what you find out about them. In general, most people in the New York theatre scene tend to be pretty liberal. It's harder to shock or offend them than someone from a theatre in a small town in some outlying area of the country.

29. "How can I make my audition really memorable?"

You have to use your creativity and imagination. An actor I know did Portia's monologue from *Julius Caesar*. It's the one where Portia is very concerned about her husband Brutus and asks him what's wrong. This woman happened to be a clown. As she was doing this very dramatic monologue, she had all these calamities happen to her, like her heel broke off on her shoe. Then she pulled on her pearls, and they went all over the floor. I thought it was really funny. But some people were worried for her. They thought she was having a really bad audition experience and asked her if she would like to try again. She was such a good actor that she convinced people that what was happening was real.

The point is you're not going to please everybody. I think that you've got to follow your instincts. Follow your heart and try to give it your best shot, based on what you do best and how you're most likely to be cast. Be creative enough to break the rules once in a while.

When I was in the movie *Sister Act*, we had already started rehearsing in LA, but there was one part that the producers couldn't cast. They had done a nationwide search, and they just couldn't find the right person for the role of the shy nun, Sister Mary Robert. She had to suddenly come out of her shell and sing like Ethel Merman. It was getting close to the time that shooting was going to begin, and they still hadn't found this person. An actor named Wendy Makkena got a call to come to audition for this role the next day. They asked her to sing a "girl group" number. For those of you who are singers, you know that isn't one of the kinds of songs you normally have at your fingertips. Not only that, Wendy didn't sing. She had never been to a singing audition.

She had twenty-four hours to get a girl group number together. She was in a total panic. She wracked her brains, trying to think of every girl group number she had ever heard. Suddenly, she remembered this Motown song called "Please Mr. Postman." The wonderful thing about it was that the verse was spoken.

She said to herself, "Great. I'll go in there. I'll speak the words. It will be like doing a monologue. I won't have to sing."

Then she remembered the chorus was sung. So she got a brilliant idea. She called up all the black women singers she knew and asked them if she could hire them to come to her audition and sing the chorus. She got four singers. They got dressed up in these tight, spangled gowns, and then they rehearsed the number that night. The next day, they all went to the audition. Wendy went in alone. She was very nervous because she was not used to going to singing auditions. All the executives from Disney were there: the producer, Scott Rudin; the screenwriter, Paul Rudnick; and all the casting directors. There must have been twenty people in the room. Wendy went up to the pianist and handed him her music. The singers were hiding in the hall.

She whispered to the accompanist, "I'm going to do the verse. When the chorus comes, give me an intro, and four women are going to burst through the door."

He looked at her and said, "Honey, it's your funeral."

But she didn't let his comments throw her. She went out, and she spoke her verse. And as planned, the four women burst into the room singing "Please Mr. Postman"! When the audition was over, the entire room stood up and cheered her. She got the part. They dubbed in her voice, so she never had to sing. Paul Rudnick later wrote about her in *The New York Times*. He said it was most brilliant audition he'd ever seen. But if she'd listened to that pianist, she might not have done so well.

Somebody at one of my seminars once said that we have become so caught up in trying to please the auditors, trying to second-guess them and do the right thing, that we've put a lid on our creativity. We've lost touch with the joy of performing. Isn't that why people go into show business, because it's fun?

I think it's really important to take risks and to go out on a limb. Yes, you might fall flat on your face. They might really not like what you do. But the alternative is that they might not remember you because you're so safe that you just kind of blend into the woodwork.

In my youth, when I was at Actor's Information Project, they were always encouraging us to do these outlandish marketing campaigns. They told us to be outrageous, and not just write the traditional cover letter, where you say "Hello, I'm an actor looking for representation." That might work in the business world, but show business is about being creative.

For my marketing campaign, I had pictures of myself as many different characters. Every week or two, I'd send a postcard as that character. I had one that looked like a hillbilly. I wrote a message about making moonshine from my still. On another postcard, I had rollers in my hair and was holding a Pekingese dog wearing matching rollers. My message talked about making clothes out of dog fur. The last postcard of this series was a picture of me with little wire-rimmed glasses and one of those fox furs where the head bites the tail. I was topless. The fox's head was going down toward my right breast and the tail heading for the left breast. I looked like this crazed librarian. So I sent out all these postcards. I was called in by an important casting director. She proceeded to scold me for sending pornographic material through the mail.

She said, "How dare you send topless pictures to me! I'm really offended by that!"

I said, "I'm sorry."

Then she said, "Well, since you're here, read for this movie I'm casting." So I did. While I was reading, she talked about me to her assistant. She said, "Do you believe her nerve sending this postcard?"

It was hard to concentrate. I just wanted to fall through the floor.

I went slinking out of there, thinking, "Why did I send those postcards? Thanks a lot for the advice, AIP."

The next day, that same casting director recommended me to her partner. He offered me a part on a major TV show. So I guess the moral is: go out on a limb! Don't be boring and safe. You've got to make them remember you.

Now, I'm not saying you should do anything illegal or dangerous. But do use your creativity, and do include yourself in it. Don't just try to be some cookie-cutter person that you think they're going to want. It's show business. So use your monologue to put on a show. An audition is very different from a job interview in the business world. There everybody's serious and grownup, wearing the gray flannel suits and being cerebral. This business is about playing. It's about having fun. If you can think of some brilliant, creative way to bring your monologue to life, like the woman doing Portia did, I say, "Go for it."

30. "Can a monologue ever be too risky?"

Yes. I would advise against doing any monologues in which you directly threaten or intimidate the auditor. I have heard of actors holding guns to auditors' heads or physically attacking them. Never touch an auditor in a threatening way. You want to make them like you and want to work with you. This kind of behavior will produce quite the opposite result.

If the character is menacing the other character in a monologue, you might take a step toward the auditors at that point, but nothing more. Also, do not touch the auditors in any kind of sexual or suggestive way. Above all, do not kiss the auditors. This may seem very obvious, but there are some actors who have crossed this line at auditions. The auditors do not want to be manhandled. If you are doing a monologue that is a love scene, just imagine the other person is there. Do not involve the auditor.

31. "Should I attend workshops where I have to pay to do monologues for agents and casting directors?"

If that's the only way you have to meet casting people, I think it is a good idea. You can also do showcases and scene nights and try to get them to come, but I think this is a lot easier and produces results. I met an agent at a paid workshop who signed me. As a result, I got a featured role in the movie *Sister Act* that provided me with five months of work on a major motion picture. So I think the $30 I paid for the workshop was definitely worth it.

I hope you will find these suggestions helpful in preparing your monologues for auditions. If you put the ideas I've discussed in this book into practice, I just know your auditions will improve.

The most important things I learned about acting came from my acting teacher, Miriam Goldina, who studied with Stanislavsky. She always told me how inspirational Stanislavsky was and how working with him ignited her passion for acting. He made her feel like she was the greatest actor in the world. That's how every one of you should feel when you go to auditions and do your monologues.

By using the techniques I've recommended, you will have a monologue that you love because it fits you like a glove, and it will express ideas that you connect with on a personal level. It will also be little known because you've gone to obscure sources to find it. And it will be acted brilliantly because you've taken the time to rehearse it thoroughly.

You can do it. You can enjoy doing monologues. Now go out there and have a great audition.

Ask the Experts

DOUG MOSER, DIRECTOR,
STAMFORD THEATREWORKS

What do you notice when an actor enters the room?

When an actor enters the room, I notice their energy. I am always interested in seeing who the person is when they enter the room because like everybody, I have a first impression. It's the same first impression I would get if I would see them at a party or on the street. It's up to me to be open to whatever person is coming into the room, but it's also up to the auditioner to be at his or her fullest self.

Do you want them to be like the character, or do you want them to be friendly and nice?

I'd rather they be friendly and nice. There is plenty of time to get the character. Also, I might be looking for something different in the character than they are coming in as.

What are some common mistakes actors make at auditions?

The most common mistake is not noticing or engaging with the people in the room. At least be happy to meet me.

How much should they engage you? I know you are on a time schedule.

They have to be able to read the room. One of the reasons I read people's resumes is I want to see what I have in common with them. I know it's a nerve-wracking experience. I am looking for a connection. Can I make that connection work?

Are there any kinds of monologues that they should avoid?

I hate ponderous ones. They are supposed to be dramatic, and the person sits in the chair and ponders some deep problem, and that gets them gazing about the room. Also, I'm one of those people who hates yelling in monologues. You should only yell when you have gone through everything else you can do. I am not interested in easy emotions. I don't like rants. I have never had a problem with an actor getting to anger in any show I have directed.

Do you have pet peeves?

I hate when a monologue is very *acted*. I like interesting choices. An actor should speak well, be heard, and be seen. You expect that. There is another level of people who are very good readers but they have no commitment. They are not bringing themselves to it. They are not revealing themselves. So they are not revealing anything about the piece, either.

Is there any type of material you like best?

No, I like to be surprised. I like bizarre sources. I can guess if it's from a monologue book. I don't really like those books. I can't stand if they don't know what it's from, or they haven't read it. They have an opportunity to interpret something, and how can you do that if you don't know the full extent? How hard is it to commit to read the play? I am more interested in the people who bring me toward them. It tells a story and brings me into it. I remember a woman doing a monologue from some weird source, and she was so committed to the moment. It was a funny monologue, but it worked because she was so committed to the seriousness of it.

JASON KASHIWAGI, AGENT, THE LUEDTKE AGENCY

What is the first thing you notice when you meet an actor?

Confidence, originality. Nice, personable, and not too over-excited. They should not act too *actory* or superficial.

What are some common mistakes actors make?

They make the easy choices. They don't take risks with their monologues. They just play it safe.

Are there any monologues that actors should avoid?

Monologues from plays that are currently on Broadway because most likely the people you are auditioning for have seen the play and have seen your monologue done better. Choose a play that's older.

Is there any type of monologue you would recommend?

It depends on each actor. If you are comedic and you find a good monologue from a sitcom, it can work wonders. It can also be disastrous. It all depends on how it's done. Monologues from plays are all about the perfect fit. Do what really showcases you. Tennessee Williams, Charles Busch are good if they aren't too well known. Find something that's strong and showcases you as an actor.

Do you remember any monologues you've seen that stand out?

Many have not been that memorable. But I liked *Angels in America, Die Mommy Die, Psycho Beach Party, Betrayal*, or if you're younger you have to look in plays for high school students.

Do you have any pet peeves?

I like to see a through line. Beginning, middle, end.

Do you like monologues from monologue books?

If they make it work, they can do almost anything. They have to sell it.

Should they look at you?

No. Look a little to the side.

How should they end the monologue?

Just pause a second and then go back into who they are. I do like them to be ready at the beginning and not take time getting into it. The most important thing is to be original, take risks, and dare to fail. Have levels, emotional colors, don't be on one level.

MARILYN SCOTT MURPHY, AGENT,
PROFESSIONAL ARTISTS

How can an actor capture your attention?

Have a strong sense of self. It's just the strength of their own personality. They come in, know who they are. Pleasant is always helpful.

What are common mistakes actors make?

Choosing material that they would not be hired to do. Stretching is for acting classes. It is more helpful if the actor has a sense of what they are right for.

Is there any kind of monologue material that you dislike?

Monologues with profanity are questionable. With some playwrights now, it's harder to stay away from it. It's not that anybody is going to be shocked by it. I think usually the situation is in such close quarters that that kind of material doesn't seem to be helpful. Mostly it doesn't particularly work. But there are no rules. If it is something that absolutely suits the person, of course it's fine.

What kind of material do you recommend?

The material should be well written. Monologues written by the actor are rarely successful, only if the actor happens to be a really good writer. I am still more inclined to think of the actor as more of an interpreter, so I'm more inclined to see how someone takes someone else's words and makes them their own.

Do you care if the monologue is well known?

It doesn't really matter, as long as the material suits the actor.

What are your pet peeves at monologue auditions?

Do not make eye contact. It takes me out of my job. My job is to watch and assess and not to feel like I'm participating in the scene. If someone makes eye contact, I am no longer the observer.

Do you remember any monologues you've seen people do that stand out?

There are two. Jan Maxwell did Nina from *The Seagull* in the fourth act. She was magnificent. Lee Brock did a monologue from *Blue Window*. Those two monologues still are the best I've ever seen people do. They are both well-known monologues, but they did them really well.

Do you have any other advice?

Pick parts you would be cast in. If you can do two mono-logues, the first should be an introductory monologue, as if the playwright had written it for you. It is pretty much who you are. I want to get to know you in it. The second one can be different—maybe with an accent. It can be comedy then serious. Mostly the first one needs to be the one that speaks from the heart.

AUSTIN PENDLETON, DIRECTOR

How can an actor make a good first impression on you?

Just by being themselves. Whether they're scared, or confi-dent, or hassled, or calm, just by being open about it and shar-ing it, not in words so much but by the way they relate to me, or whoever is in the room.

What type of material should an actor choose for his or her monologue?

Select monologues that they can work on. Where they can read the whole play (not the kind in monologue books where the whole play can't be found anywhere) and can work on the whole play, so that the monologue is not just something torn from its branches. And monologues that not everybody uses. And mono-logues they personally relate to. These don't have to be specific to the actor's personal life, of course. Just something that gets them going.

What are some common mistakes actors make?

Common mistake: they're not talking TO anybody in their imagination. They're internalizing everything. There's no imme-diacy in the present moment. Almost any monologue is some-thing actually said to somebody else in the play, for a particular reason, at that moment, not something that's said just to relive the past or dredge up some pre-existing emotional state. So the actor should select something on the back wall, a light switch, a little hole-in-the-wall anything, and talk to it as if it were the person their character is talking to at that moment, and hope that maybe they can affect that thing on the wall, and make it do what they want, and get really invested in that.

DAVID ELLIOTT, AGENT, DON BUCHWALD AGENCY

When you first meet an actor, how can they get your attention immediately?

I think people need to be on from the moment they walk in the door. The entire meeting is really an audition. You see what the person is like and how they are going to be to work with, so from the second they walk in, it should be an up kind of thing.

What are some common mistakes actors make at monologue auditions?

People finish their performance abruptly. If they jarringly cut it off, it breaks the moment and it weakens what the performance was. Take a moment to be there at the end. Pause.

Is there any material to avoid?

Overly personal stuff is not necessarily good. Sometimes people perform that stuff well. But in the back of my head I'm thinking, "Are they doing it well because it really happened to them and of course it's coming off as real, or are they really talented and if they were given different material, could they do it as well?"

Do you recommend any particular type of material?

In general, people should do something that's close to who they are. Particularly if you are meeting someone for the first time, don't come in and do some wacky character that's not what you're like or you would ever be hired for just because you want to stretch. Give me a sense of who you are and what you are like.

What are your pet peeves?

When people end abruptly. When they do things on one level—like if they are angry or some other emotion all the way through. It's not showing anything. I want to see rises and falls, peaks and valleys, subtlety. I want to see the opposite of what I expect.

One thing I remember an agent named Pat House told an actor years ago. She said, "Always look for the love and look for the humor." I would add to that, always do the opposite of the obvious.

ANTHONY MCKAY, ACTING FACULTY, DRAMA DEPT., CARNEGIE MELLON UNIVERSITY

What can an actor do to capture your attention when he enters the room?

I don't think that should be the goal when an actor enters a room. It is their moment to just be themselves before they go about their business. To demand that the actor rivet my attention during an initial greeting would, I think, distort the whole audition process.

After doing literally thousand of auditions for CMU, what I want is someone to come in with some self-possession: polite, present but while making eye contact and giving me a good handshake. (I always shake their hand to see what their handshake is like. Somehow I feel I can tell something about them through their grip or lack of it.) They are concentrated on the job at hand.

What are some common mistakes actors make at monologue auditions?

One of the commonest for young actors at least is finishing up too early: the last word is said and they look at me for response. This means to me that their connection to their imaginary partner was not strong, and their focus was on me throughout and not the purposes of their monologue.

Asking to start over again. I can't remember a monologue that was restarted and got better. It is, in fact, more interesting to see an actor struggle through his or her difficulties; it shows some fiber and sometimes nets interesting results.

What types of monologues should they avoid?

Reflective monologues or memory monologues that trod down memory lane; they tend to pull the actor in and emphasize the general mood. Not exciting stuff.

Also, story monologues, while they can be effective, don't tell me much about the performer. And I confess that I am sometimes at a loss as to how to direct them if I want to see more. I usually try and redirect the monologue so that it has a strong objective: Now you're telling it to the police to clear yourself of murder! But the point is a monologue should put the actor on top of a hot-plate where the character's needs are coming out the actor's ears. A story monologue tends to be pre-organized and sedate without many surprises.

What types do you recommend?

Active monologues: speeches that are directed at someone from whom they need something desperately and need it now.

Plus, monologues they really relate to. Monologues that say something about them and let me know who they are. And that let me see that in their choice of monologue they have a good idea of how they would be cast or what their strong suit is.

It is really disconcerting to see a pretty ingénue take on "Out damn spot!" I think, perhaps unfairly, she really is out of touch.

What do you look for in a monologue audition?

Who the actor is. I don't want anything to get in the way of my getting to know that actor/person. That's why the choice of material is so important. Does it show off the actor's strength?

Also, and primary, do they connect with the material or are they performing. The rooms mostly in hotels where I do my auditioning are intimate (I'm only fifteen feet away from them), and it is discernable in a moment if the actor is whipping up a storm to hide a lack of connection to the material.

And, also important, are they flexible and game. I inevitably throw an adjustment at them to see if they are thinking on their feet or are merely programmed. Their response to my direction is always very telling.

The two stipulations above are why I don't recommend that actors come into the room trying to overwhelm me with their charm and robust personality. I recommend they stay within themselves, keeping in touch with that center that will serve them in the audition.

I realize as I am writing this I am talking strictly about monologue auditions and not the kind of audition when you are preparing a part from a script. I hope that's helpful to you.

Any pet peeves?

People who try and charm too much before the audition. Keep it polite but businesslike. It's very different from an interview.

Actors who get closer and closer in the course of their monologue as if the decrease in the distance between auditor and the actor increases the intensity of the acting. It does just the opposite; it makes the person or persons watching the audition uncomfortable, and secondly, it is a desperation move born of emptiness.

Any general advice?

Try and pick pieces that are close to you that stir you and that stay within the parameters in which you would be cast.

Monologues They Never Want to Hear Again

Female

A . . . My Name Is Alice
Anything by Sam Shepard
Blue Window
Brilliant Traces
Butterflies Are Free
Cat on a Hot Tin Roof
The Colored Museum
Crimes of the Heart
Danny and the Deep Blue Sea
The Days and Nights of Beebee
    Fenstermaker
'Dentity Crisis
Father's Day
Fences
Getting Out
The Glass Menagerie
It Had to Be You
Kennedy's Children
Laughing Wild (tuna fish
    monologue)
Little Murders
Marco Polo Sings a Solo
The Marriage of Bette and Boo
Nuts
Painting Churches
Savage in Limbo
Say Good Night, Gracie
The Sign in Sidney Brustein's
    Window
Slow Dance on the Killing
    Ground
The Star-Spangled Girl
A Streetcar Named Desire
Talking With
Uncommon Women and Others
Whiskey
Women of Manhattan
The Woolgatherer

Male

Ah, Wilderness!
All My Sons
Angels in America
Anything by Sam Shepard
A Boy's Life
Brighton Beach Memoirs
Burn This
Danny and the Deep Blue Sea
The Dark at the Top of the Stairs
Death of a Salesman
Does a Tiger Wear a Necktie?
Equus
The Fantasticks
The Glass Menagerie

Glengarry Glen Ross
Hello, Dolly!
I Hate Hamlet
I Never Sang for My Father
Key Exchange
Long Day's Journey into Night
Lovers and Other Strangers
Of the Fields Lately
P.S. Your Cat Is Dead

Private Wars
The Rainmaker
Short Eyes
Six Degrees of Separation
Spoon River Anthology
Talley's Folly
A Thousand Clowns
Tracers
Who's Afraid of Virginia Woolf?

Your Audition Diary

Every actor should carry around a journal on himself or herself.

Many times, people will say things like, "Oh, you look like so and so" or "Were you in this movie?"

Those comments are good little bits of information that will help you to figure out your type. But if you don't write them down, you might forget them. As I have said, you are your product, so you want every bit of information on yourself you can get. That's why I've provided this audition diary for you to use at auditions. Fill it out after each audition. Review it often. You'll learn so much.

AUDITION DIARY

DATE:

TIME:

PLACE:

MONOLOGUE USED:

CLOTHING WORN:

AUDITORS PRESENT:

FEEDBACK:

HOW DID YOU FEEL?

AUDITION DIARY

DATE:

TIME:

PLACE:

MONOLOGUE USED:

CLOTHING WORN:

AUDITORS PRESENT:

FEEDBACK:

HOW DID YOU FEEL?

AUDITION DIARY

DATE:

TIME:

PLACE:

MONOLOGUE USED:

CLOTHING WORN:

AUDITORS PRESENT:

FEEDBACK:

HOW DID YOU FEEL?

AUDITION DIARY

DATE:

TIME:

PLACE:

MONOLOGUE USED:

CLOTHING WORN:

AUDITORS PRESENT:

FEEDBACK:

HOW DID YOU FEEL?

AUDITION DIARY

DATE:

TIME:

PLACE:

MONOLOGUE USED:

CLOTHING WORN:

AUDITORS PRESENT:

FEEDBACK:

HOW DID YOU FEEL?

AUDITION DIARY

DATE:

TIME:

PLACE:

MONOLOGUE USED:

CLOTHING WORN:

AUDITORS PRESENT:

FEEDBACK:

HOW DID YOU FEEL?

AUDITION DIARY

DATE:

TIME:

PLACE:

MONOLOGUE USED:

CLOTHING WORN:

AUDITORS PRESENT:

FEEDBACK:

HOW DID YOU FEEL?

AUDITION DIARY

DATE:

TIME:

PLACE:

MONOLOGUE USED:

CLOTHING WORN:

AUDITORS PRESENT:

FEEDBACK:

HOW DID YOU FEEL?

AUDITION DIARY

DATE:

TIME:

PLACE:

MONOLOGUE USED:

CLOTHING WORN:

AUDITORS PRESENT:

FEEDBACK:

HOW DID YOU FEEL?

AUDITION DIARY

DATE:

TIME:

PLACE:

MONOLOGUE USED:

CLOTHING WORN:

AUDITORS PRESENT:

FEEDBACK:

HOW DID YOU FEEL?

AUDITION DIARY

DATE:

TIME:

PLACE:

MONOLOGUE USED:

CLOTHING WORN:

AUDITORS PRESENT:

FEEDBACK:

HOW DID YOU FEEL?

Bibliography

Brontë, Charlotte. *Jane Eyre*. The Literature Network. http://www
.online-literature.com/brontec/janeeyre.

Brontë, Emily. *Wuthering Heights*. The Literature Network. http://
www.online-literature.com/bronte/wuthering.

Chekhov, Anton. *Ivanov*. Translated by Marian Fell. New York:
Charles Scribner's Sons, 1912.

Masters, Edgar Lee. *Spoon River Anthology*. New York: The Macmillan
Company, 1916; Bartleby.com, 1999. www.bartleby.com/84/.

Shakespeare, William. *Henry VI, Part I*. The Complete Works of
William Shakespeare. http://shakespeare.mit.edu/1henryvi/
full.html.

———. *The Taming of the Shrew*. The Complete Works of William
Shakespeare. http://shakespeare.mit.edu/taming_shrew/full
.html.

About the Author

PRUDENCE WRIGHT HOLMES has been coaching actors for over twenty-five years. Her students have appeared in films, television, on and off-Broadway, regional theatres, and commercials. She has taught at the Carnegie Mellon Drama Department, the NYU Drama Department, the Actors Studio at the New School, and the American Academy of Dramatic Arts. She has given workshops at the Mason Gross School of the Arts at Rutgers University, the Neighborhood Playhouse, the Strasberg Institute, the Actor's Connection, Weist Baron, AFTRA, and the Screen Actor's Guild. She is the author of *Voices of Thinking Jewish Women*.

Holmes, who has been called "the Monologue Detective," knows from personal experience how to choose and perform monologues that get jobs. She has appeared in featured roles in the films *Sister Act* and *Sister Act 2* with Whoopi Goldberg, *Kingpin* with Woody Harrelson, *In Dreams* with Annette Bening, *My Own Love Song* with Renee Zellweger, *After.Life* with Liam Neeson, and *Boardwalk Empire* with Steve Buscemi. On Broadway she appeared in *Happy End* with Meryl Streep, *Lettice and Lovage* with Maggie Smith, *Inherit the Wind* with George C. Scott, and *The Light in the Piazza* at Lincoln Center and on the national tour. She has appeared in numerous off-Broadway shows, including the original casts of *Godspell* and *Sister Mary Ignatius Explains It All for You*. She wrote and performed her solo show *Bexley, Oh!*, about her hometown of Bexley, Ohio, at New York Theatre Workshop.